Endpapers, front: *The waves in Maldives are safe for surfing; surfers are a common sight off the eastern corner of Male.*
Endpapers, back: *Phosphorus glistens as a dhoni ploughs through the sea at sunset.*
Pages 2-3: *Boats (dhonis) like these are the taxis of the islands.*
Page 4: *An aerial view of the southernmost island of Gan in Addu Atoll.*
Page 6: *A youthful welcome for visitors.*
Page 8: *Inter-island* dhoni *under repair.*

Vorsatzblätter, Vorderseite: *Die Wellen vor den Küsten der Malediven sind ungefährlich und zum Surfen bestens geeignet; Surfer vor der Ostküste Males sind ein alltäglicher Anblick.*
Vorsatzblätter, Rückseite: *Das Meer glänzt silbrig, während ein* Dhoni *im Sonnenuntergang vorbeigleitet.*
Seiten 2-3: *Boote (Dhonis) dieser Art fungieren als Taxis zwischen den Inseln.*
Seite 4: *Ein Blick aus der Vogelperspektive auf die Insel Gan am südlichsten Ende des Addu-Atolls.*
Seite 6: *Besucher werden mit jugendlichem Überschwang begrüßt.*
Seite 8: *Ein zwischen den Inseln verkehrendes* Dhoni *wird repariert.*

Prima di copertina: *Le onde alle Maldive sono sicure per il surf; si vedono parecchi surfisti al largo della punta orientale di Malè.*
Ultima di copertina: *Il fosforo luccica al passaggio di una* dhoni *sul mare, al tramonto.*
Pagine 2-3: *Imbarcazioni (dhonis) come queste sono i taxi delle isole.*
Pagina 4: *Una veduta aerea dell'isola più meridionale, Gan nell'atollo di Addu.*
Pagina 6: *Un giovane benvenuto ai turisti.*
Pagina 8: *Una* dhoni *interinsulare in riparazione.*

© 1997 Ministry of Tourism, Republic of Maldives
© 1997 Times Editions, Singapore
All photographs copyrighted Gemunu Amarasinghe except where otherwise stated

Published for the Ministry of Tourism, Republic of Maldives
by Times Editions
an imprint of Times Editions Pte Ltd
Times Centre, 1 New Industrial Road
Singapore 536196

Project Editor: K E Tan
Designed by Felicia Wong
Colour separation by Colourscan Co. Pte Ltd, Singapore
Printed in Malaysia

ISBN 981 204 767 0

With compliments
from.
Bandos Island Resort.
Maldives.

A Maldives Celebration

To: Mr. & Mrs. Burchell.
Room: 165

ACCESS FOR FIRE
EXTINGUISHING

A Maldives Celebration

Written by
ROYSTON ELLIS

Photographed by
GEMUNU AMARASINGHE

Published for the MINISTRY OF TOURISM, REPUBLIC OF MALDIVES by TIMES EDITIONS

Contents

Acknowledgements

There are people met casually with whom it is possible to establish an immediate rapport, even if you don't have much in common. Maldivians are like that, responding to visitors with a genuine, albeit shy, charm that contributes to making the Maldives more than just a delightful tourist destination; for many visitors, the yearn to return becomes a passion.

I have been lucky enough to return to the Maldives many times since tourism was in its infancy, and each time I discover new facets of this gem of an archipelago. So many Maldivians have helped Gemunu Amarasinghe and myself gain insights into the unique character and beauty of the Maldives, we regret it is impossible to thank everyone of them by name.

To His Excellency, Maumoon Abdul Gayoom, President of the Republic of Maldives, we are indebted for the time he spent answering our questions and for helping us to understand more about the islands. To the Minister of Tourism, the Hon. Ibrahim Hussain Zaki, we are grateful for the support given to us in developing this idea into a book; and to Abdulla Saeed, Deputy Director, Marketing and Research, Ministry of Tourism, and his staff, thanks for the personal interest they took in this project.

To Shaahina and Gert of Sea Explorers Diving School thanks for the underwater photographs on pages 74-78. The photographs on pages 12 and 28 are reproduced by courtesy of the National Council of Linguistic and Cultural Research, Male', while those on pages 53, 56 and 60 are reproduced by courtesy of the Ministry of Tourism, Male'. The old stamps on page 114 are from the collection of Mr M. H. Manik. The First Day Cover on page 114 and the map reproduced on page 10 come from my own collection of Maldives memorabilia.

Royston Ellis, Male', 1997

Cadenio Quilsa *Male *Talicheri Calicut

Laquedives Deypour Tator

Ameni MALABAR Scheringhan

Maripida Aquelao Trichenapali Tanjadur

Eacondi Caratoli Cranganor

Palicar

Seukelpar Calpini Cochin Madur

Maligue Porca Tinucurin

Cul̃an

Kelay Anjinga Trangancor

Coleschey Colete Colo

*C. Comorin Côte la Perherie

Détila Molle Atol Quilai G. de Manc Cal

Sanra

Deticoa Marcomode Co

Malindo

Mandon

Adali Point

Male Mondot Atol Atol de Padipet

Galle

Maldiva Atol

*Isles Male *Maldives DE

Avic Atol L. du Roy

Brisso d'Artot

Feled oasse Atol

Anadou

Melendi Atol Atol de Mulaca

Atol de Colmondo

D.

200 222 Atol de Aldumali

de 25 au D

130 125

o au D.

100

LIGNE Atol de Sua Diva

EQUINOCT

A Welcome Tradition

The Background of History

Sailing on an azure sea, eastwards to the rising sun, vessels from Arabia and Africa would have chanced on islands barely visible beyond the surging of waves on the reefs around them. Other ships, just as fragile, chased westwards by monsoon winds under clouds glowering with gloom would have found welcome shelter in the calmer waters of the island lagoons.

Perhaps the first visitors to the Maldives arrived through nature's whims, borne by kindly currents or, storm-tossed and exhausted, in need of refuge. Word of the islands, of their bounteous waters and shell-lined, palm-fringed shores, would have been spread by seafarers; tales that must have encouraged spirited adventurers to seek out the Maldive Islands for themselves. The Maldives, before history records their early years, would have been an idyllic, peaceful haven for all who found their way there.

The first settlers would have come from many nations; from what was Arabia and Egypt, and from Malaysia and Indonesia and, by design rather than happenstance, from India and Sri Lanka. With them came their culture and beliefs.

There is architectural evidence that Buddhists and Hindus settled in some islands. It seems logical that, since many travellers came from Arabia, Islam was the faith of many settlers long before its official acceptance as the religion of all the islands.

From the darkness of legend it is possible to discern that the island communities descended from seafarers who decided to stay, had little time for disputes. Survival, from the sea and modest agriculture, was more important. There were enough islands for those who wanted to leave, to go and live on another one. Gradually, a nation of island came into being. Male'—probably because of its location in the centre of the atolls—assumed the importance of a capital.

The people of the Maldives have always welcomed visitors warmly. Legend suggests that a couple of royal blood arrived in the island of Rasgetheemu from what is now Sri Lanka. They were welcomed so royally, they were persuaded to remain. Thus began the dynasty which was, due to the influence of another visitor, to make Islam the religion of the realm, and to change it to a Sultanate.

That visitor was a traveller from Morocco, known as Abul Barakaath Yousuf Al

FACING PAGE
Detail from a map by Bonne, Paris, 1780.

GEGENÜBERLIEGENDE SEITE
Ausschnitt aus einer Karte von Bonne, Paris 1780.

PAGINA A FRONTE
Dettaglio da una mappa di Bonne, Parigi, 1780

Barbary. Few visitors who came in peace to any country could have had such an impact on a population.

To placate a demon of the sea called Rannamarai who threatened to destroy Male', it was the custom to leave a virgin for him in the temple at night on the first day of every month. The next morning the girl would be found dead.

Abul Barakaath was a Muslim. He took the girl's place in the temple and began reciting verses from the Holy Koran. The demon was overwhelmed. It sank back to the sea, never to return. Abul Barakaath was regarded with such awe his faith was decreed as the saviour of the Maldives.

Archaeologist H. C. P. Bell records the conversion to Islam of the islands less romantically in his Monograph based on his visits in the 1920s:

"Muslim predominance, enhanced steadily by regular trade and commerce in the course of three or four centuries at least, culminated in the overthrow of Buddhism, the ruling religion of the Group, and the conversion of the Islands to Islam in the mid twelfth century."

Islam was officially declared the religion in 1153. The king became the Sultan, beginning a series of dynasties that prevailed for over 800 years, until 1968, despite many attempts at invasion and, in 1953, a year's experiment as a republic.

As the Maldives became unified in faith and as a Sultanate, the islands attracted more visitors from overseas. To the Chinese, they were regarded as the "Three Thousand Weak Waters".

To the Portuguese, the Maldives were islands to be secured in their quest for supremacy of the sea. As the first visitors to the Maldives who did not come in peace, their invasion was resisted heroically, but unsuccessfully, by Sultan Ali VI, in 1558. The Portuguese stayed to inflict a reign of terror—in the name of Christianity—until the brave guerrilla warfare tactics of the Maldives' hero who became Sultan Ghaazee Muhammad Thakurufaanu, liberated the islands after 15 years.

South Indian pirates and expeditions of Malabar opportunists tried to conquer the Maldives and 13 wars were fought in the 17th century to preserve the islands' independence. The Dutch, who held neighbouring Ceylon, were interested in the Maldives as a source of trade, mainly the cowrie shells which were in demand as currency. They surveyed the islands of the Maldives and Laccadives in 1671 but never tried to invade.

A defence treaty with the French, who had a fort at Pondicherry on India's southern coast, helped the Maldives repel more Malabar adventurers. This did not lead to a lasting French connection. As British naval influence spread through the Indian Ocean, the sultans of the Maldives shrewdly maintained cordial relations without allowing the British to settle. A survey of the islands was begun in 1834 by the Royal Navy; it is the foundation of the maritime charts in use even now.

There was an exchange of letters between the governor of the then British-ruled Ceylon, representing Queen Victoria, and the Sultan of the Maldives in 1887. This had the effect of keeping the British at bay while acknowledging their influence over the Indian Ocean. The statehood of the Maldives was recognised and Britain had no power to interfere in internal matters, although they did control

external affairs and regarded the Maldives as a protected state.

It was not until 1932 that a written constitution was formulated. This was largely based on the customs, conventions and other traditional administrative practices that had been followed for centuries. A form of democracy always existed with systems of taxation, national defence and justice. The post of Sultan—or Sultana, for sometimes a woman was chosen as ruler—was not hereditary and each ruler's actions were closely monitored by various councils who could—and did—depose a ruler who exceeded his power.

The constitution was amended several times, with the adoption of the Sixth Constitution resulting in the creation of the First Republic, with a presidency replacing the sultanate in 1953. The Republic was short-lived and the Sultanate restored.

Mohamed Ameen Didi, formerly prime minister, was the first president and has been judged by history as a founding father of modern Maldives, particularly for his reform of the education system, reviving the Maldivian language and literature, and giving women more of a place in society. He died following unrest and is buried on the island of Vihamanaafushi that became the first tourist resort: Kurumba.

Full independence returned to the Maldives in 1965 with an agreement ending Britain's role signed by the then prime minister, Ibrahim Nasir and the British High Commissioner in Ceylon. The Maldives became a member of the United Nations in 1965, and a full member of the Commonwealth of Nations in 1985. The Tenth Constitution led to the replacement of the Sultanate and the creation of the current

ABOVE
*Entrance to the shrine of
Muhammad Thakurufaanu,
adjoining the Male' residence
built for a former Sultan.*

OBEN
*Eingang zum Schrein
Muhammad Thakurufaanu,
angrenzend die für einen
früheren Sultan erbaute
Residenz in Male.*

SOPRA
*Entrata al tempio di Muhammad
Thakurufaanu, aggiunto alla
residenza di Malè costruita per
un Sultano precedente.*

Republic in 1968 with Ibrahim Nasir as president.

The president is nominated by the Citizens' Majlis (a parliament of 40 elected members and eight presidential appointees), and elected at a presidential referendum held every five years.

In 1978 a former lecturer in Islamic Studies and Philosophy who became the Maldives' permanent representative to the United Nations and a government minister, Maumoon Abdul Gayoom, was elected as president. He was returned to office for a fourth term in 1993.

Although the Maldives began to be known as an idyllic holiday destination at the beginning of the 1970s, it was not until President Gayoom was elected that the significance of the tourism industry to the Maldives was realised. During his successive terms of office, development and prosperity have increased in a manner that was unimaginable 20 years ago.

The success of tourism has enabled the nation to meet the aspirations of its citizens. The welcome visitors feel when they arrive derives from the simple charm inspired by the faith and independent spirit of a devout and industrious island people.

As visitors to the Maldives have increased over 25 years, from 1,097 in 1972 to an estimated 400,000 in 1997, so, too, has the consequences of tourism. The very nature of the Maldives, with each resort on its own, dedicated island, prevents the havoc large numbers of foreign visitors could wreak on local society.

The Maldives is fortunate in being blessed not only by nature's endowments but also by visitors who respect the nation's religion, culture and traditions. Visitors share in the treasures of the Maldives, contributing to the islands' well-being and progress, while finding a holiday fulfillment rare in the modern, stress-filled world.

It was not just a jubilee celebrated in 1997, but a year-long paean to the people who make the Maldives, and a holiday among them, so memorable.

FACING PAGE
Watched by the President and ministers and members of the diplomatic corps (top left), schoolchildren commemorate Independence Day with drill displays (top right) and participation in a pageant (bottom).

GEGENÜBERLIEGENDE SEITE
Unter den wachsamen Blicken des Präsidenten sowie Ministern und Mitgliedern des diplomatischen Corps (links oben) feiern Schulkinder den Unabhängigkeitstag mit Paraden (rechts oben) und Festzügen (unten).

PAGINA A FRONTE
Sotto lo sguardo del Presidente, dei ministri e dei membri del corpo diplomatico (in alto a sinistra), gli studenti commemorano il Giorno dell'Indipendenza con parate (in alto a destra) e partecipando ad uno spettacolo.

Visit Maldives Year

It was planned three years before: a yearlong celebration of the 25th anniversary of the start of the tourist industry, with 1997 being declared Visit Maldives Year.

Internationally, celebrations to mark the event were tied in with tourism trade fairs and road shows in Germany, Italy, England and Japan. Nationally, every resort began planning in 1996 for the special events to be held in their islands. These ranged from every tourist planting a coconut tree in some resorts, to reef and lagoon cleaning in others, with beauty pageants, sports competitions and culinary exhibitions as additional attractions.

The Ministry of Tourism created a programme of activities beginning with a New Year Theme Toast and Tourism Fiesta in Male' at the start of 1997. Included were a World Tourism Organisation conference on the environment, an art and essay competition for school children, football matches, tourism theme floats for the Independence Day parade, an international diving conference, and an arts, graphic and photography exhibition.

Getting to Know the Maldives

Money Matters: Nature's Mint

Few visitors realise today that the Maldives had an influence on world affairs for over 1,000 years. The importance of the island sultanate was due to a shining, tiny shell: the cowrie.

The cowrie was one of the world's trading currencies throughout the Middle Ages up to 300 years ago. The presence of this small, white mollusk (*Cyprea moneta*) in Maldives' lagoons and on the beaches was a great lure for traders. It won worldwide renown for the islands.

Cowries from the Maldives have been dug up in Finland and even on the Atlantic coast north of the Arctic Circle. They have also been found on the coast of the Caspian Sea where merchants would have obtained them from Arab traders.

The value of a cowrie fluctuated. According to Ibn Batuta, during 1344 one dinar in the Maldives could be exchanged for 400,000 cowries, while in Sudan, a gold dinar was needed to buy 1,150 cowries. In the 17th century, according to Pyrard, one dollar, or piece of eight, was the cost of 60,000 cowries.

As the use of shells for currency diminished, cowries were replaced in the Maldives by money fashioned from silver wire and looking rather like a hairpin. The first *Digu Laari* (long laari) minted in the Maldives is believed to have been introduced between 1575 and 1600. The first round laari was produced in 1663. Currency from India and Ceylon was used, promoted by the presence of merchants and traders from those countries.

The Maldives Rufiayaa was introduced in 1948. Paper currency had to be used due to the escalating volume of cash business of the foreign traders and, thus, the increasing need for large sums of money.

The era of barter and the cowrie shell had finally succumbed to the world of more ruthless commerce. Now cowries are only exchanged for money in souvenir shops but visitors can still find them on resort island beaches. Many however prefer to leave them where they are.

FACING PAGE
Nature has blessed the Maldives with hundreds of beautiful islands where palm trees shade beaches caressed by the gentle waters of a blue lagoon.

GEGENÜBERLIEGENDE SEITE
Die Malediven mit ihren Hunderten wunderschöner Inseln sind ein Geschenk der Natur; Palmen spenden Schatten für die Strände dieser Inseln, die vom Wasser blauer Lagunen zart umspült werden.

PAGINA A FRONTE
La natura ha donato alle Maldive centinaia di splendide isole dove le palme ombreggiano spiagge accarezzate dalle calme acque di una laguna blu.

The Nation's Emblems

The National Emblem, to be seen on government publications and as a shield on the wrought iron railings of the President's Palace (Theemuge) consists of a central, stylised coconut palm tree and a crescent embracing a five-pointed star, with the national flag at each side.

The coconut palm is honoured because of the role it plays in island life. Its wood is used for building both houses and boats, its palm leaves for thatching and fencing, its sap when extracted as toddy is a nutritious thirst quencher, the shell of its nuts can be used as containers while their flesh is an important ingredient for cooking. Even the husk's fibre is used for rope or mattress filling.

The national flower is *Finifenmaa*, commonly known as the Pink Rose (*Rosa polyantha*). It is adored by Maldivians even though it is not typical of tropical islands where bougainvillaea and hibiscus flourish more heartily.

The national flag is red, green and white. A green rectangle denoting life, progress and prosperity, has a white crescent at its centre to represent the Islamic faith of the nation. The red border around the green rectangle symbolises the blood of the national heroes shed for the independence and sovereignty of the nation.

Secret Language

The language of the Maldives is known as Dhivehi, and the Maldivians themselves are Dhivehin. In Dhivehi, the Maldives is known as Dhivehi Raajje (Realm of the Dhivehin). It is written from right to left in a script that is unique to the Maldives and is called *Thaana*.

Dhivehi can best be described as an Indo-Aryan language with influences of Sinhala, Hindi, Arabic and Bengali, although its development, since it was spoken by isolated islanders, was independent of the mainstream.

It is probable that, in order to preserve their identity, islanders deliberately adapted words they borrowed, to form a secret language incomprehensible to outsiders. It helped in the development of an individual culture and encouraged filtering of influences so that only what was relevant to island life at the time was retained.

To the visitor, some words sound engagingly familiar. That is because English has infiltrated too, supplying words not at first needed. Thus you might open a *dhoru* to get into your hotel room, or visit a *daktaru* if you are sick. The borrowing of words has not been entirely a one-way process. From the Maldivian word *atholhu*, English has adapted *atoll* to describe a ring-shaped coral reef of islands encircling a lagoon.

FACING PAGE
Cowrie shells (top left) were used as currency until the introduction of coins (bottom) in the 17th century. Top centre: Dhivehi script reading: "A Maldives Celebration". Top right: The national flag flies above Jumhooree Maidan, close to the presidential jetty.

GEGENÜBERLIEGENDE SEITE
Kaurimuscheln (links oben) wurden bis zur Einführung von Münzgeld im 17. Jahrhundert als Zahlungsmittel verwendet. Mitte oben: Dhivehi-Schrift mit folgendem Wortlaut: "Ein Fest der Malediven". Rechts oben: Die Nationalflagge ist über dem Jumhooree-Maidan (Marktplatz) nahe dem Anleger des Präsidenten gehißt.

PAGINA A FRONTE
Le conchiglie sono state usate come denaro fino all'introduzione delle monete (sotto) nel 17esimo secolo. Sopra, al centro: Una scritta Dhivehi che dice: "Una celebrazione delle Maldive". Sopra, a destra: La bandiera nazionale sventola su Jumhooree Maidan, vicino al molo presidenziale.

Atoll Story

Atolls give the Maldives its landmass. There are 26 natural atolls, every one formed by a coral reef with a reef and shallow lagoon encircling each island within the atoll's waters. Only about 298 square kilometres (115 square miles) of the Republic's area of approximately 89,976 square kilometres (34,740 square miles) is land, with the sea forming over 99% of its territory. The Maldives is not the smallest nation on earth in terms of size or population but it is the most watery.

The number of islands in the Maldives is the subject of endless arguments. Marco Polo (1254-1324) speculated 12,000, while a volume of the *Encyclopaedia Britannica* insists the Maldives has 1,087 islands. The official figure is 1,190 but Maldivians like to talk of 2,000 islands.

The archipelago has 198 inhabited islands (200 for official purposes). It extends as a slender chain from 7° above the Equator (latitude 7° 6' 30" north) to just beyond it (0° 41' 48" south) with India and Sri Lanka the nearest neighbours to the east. It covers 822 kilometres north to south and is 130 kilometres at its widest.

For the visitor the islands are typical of a tropical dream: swaying coconut palms and soft, white sandy beaches lapped by the gentle surf of lagoons with water so clear you can see the rainbow hues of shoals of fish swimming close to the shore. Coral reefs protect low-lying islands (only one island reaches 6 metres or 20 feet above sea level) and create its enchantment of lagoons; beyond the reefs the sea deepens to more than 200 fathoms.

Nearly a quarter of a million people live on the islands. The people are of a rich and mixed ancestry and display prominent Aryan, Dravidian, Negroid, Arab and Mongaloid features. The country is 100% Sunni Muslim.

Of the 198 inhabited islands, Male', the capital, is the most populated with about 63,000 people living in its approximately two square kilometre area. Other islands have populations ranging from 200 to 3,000.

Even the islands classed as uninhabited have residents. This is because holiday resorts are only built on uninhabited islands. They have a transient population of staff from other inhabited islands as well as expatriate staff and their guests from abroad. By the end of 1996 there were 74 resort islands, with a resort on Gan (the southernmost island), four hotels in Male', some guesthouses and a fleet of about 87 safari boats: a total of more than 12,700 beds for tourists.

The Maldives is ideal for visitors throughout the year and the tourist season is considered yearlong. While visitors from Europe holiday during the bleak winter months of the north, tourists from the Southern Hemisphere prefer the islands' summer months, April to September. August is always a popular time, June the least, perhaps because of the monsoon. It does rain in the Maldives and tropical showers are more likely during the period of the southwest monsoon, May to October.

There are hot days and cooler nights (and the skies bluer and the air more invigorating) during the dry, northeast monsoon, at its best January to March. On average over a year, there are nearly eight hours of sunshine a day. The daily maximum temperature is 30.3° C; minimum 25.3° C.

Any time is good to visit. In the Maldives, summer seems to last all year.

REPUBLIC OF MALDIVES

NORTHERN ATOLLS

INDIAN OCEAN

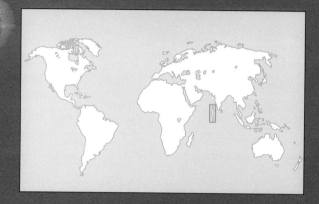

Haa Alif Atoll

Haa Dhaal Atoll

Shaviyani Atoll

Noonu Atoll

Raa Atoll

Kuredhdhu •

Lhaviyani Atoll

Baa Atoll

• **Kunfunadhoo**

North Male'
(Kaaf) Atoll

International Airport

MALE'

Alif (Ari) Atoll

South Male'
(Kaaf) Atoll

Dhiggiri
Alimatha

Vaavu Atoll

Faaf Atoll

Meemu Atoll

Dhaal Atoll

SOUTHERN ATOLLS

Thaa Atoll

Laamu Atoll

INDIAN OCEAN

Gaaf Alif Atoll

Gaaf Dhaal Atoll

N

KEY

⬚ Atolls with resort islands

• Resorts in other atolls

Gnaviyani Atoll

Seenu (Addu) Atoll
Gan

Equator

A Star Is Born:
Tourism Brightly Shines

Feel the Quality

If there is a single watchword governing the development of tourism in the Maldives, it is QUALITY.

"If we wanted tourism in quantity," said Ibrahim Hussain Zaki, the Minister of Tourism, "we could easily do it. With over 1,000 uninhabited islands only 73 of them are holiday resorts, so we have plenty of islands to develop."

Mass tourism is not seen as compatible with the Maldives. However, the Maldives does not plan to become so exclusive that a holiday there is put beyond the reach of most visitors. The aim is to provide all tourists with a holiday that is good value as well as enjoyable; that is an experience of quality.

Since being appointed as Minister of Tourism in 1993, Ibrahim Hussain Zaki has been at the forefront of changes in the industry. "Tourism in the Maldives has matured," he said. "It brings in 70% of the country's foreign exchange, earns 40% of government revenue and contributes almost 20% of the GDP. Its success has been due to planning and keeping to certain standards. Its continued success depends a lot on marketing."

The strategy employed by the Tourism Ministry is to make the world know of the Maldives as a single destination, not as individual island resorts. Only then can the impact of the Maldives as the perfect place for a holiday register properly. To achieve this, the Ministry and the industry work closely together in promoting the Maldives. The setting up of the Maldives Tourist Promotion Board, with industry participation, is part of the government's new approach.

Minister Zaki has spoken of the excellent consultative relationship his ministry enjoys with the Maldives Association of Tourism Industry (MATI), which is seen by both as beneficial to both. "It would be difficult to talk with every hotelier individually," said the Minister. "We appreciate MATI's experience."

The Minister attributes the success of the Maldives' tourism to its planned development. "Tourism has not been allowed to develop haphazardly. We always have a masterplan."

FACING PAGE
To preserve the natural, rustic look, the palm thatch roofs of guest cottages on a resort island are renewed every year.

GEGENÜBERLIEGENDE SEITE
Die mit Palmenblättern gedeckten Dächer der Gästehäuser auf einer Hotelinsel werden jedes Jahr erneuert, um die ursprüngliche, rurale Atmosphäre der Inseln zu bewahren.

PAGINA A FRONTE
Per conservarne l'aspetto naturale e rustico, i tetti di palma delle capanne di un complesso turistico sono rinnovati ogni anno.

In 1996, the cabinet accepted most of the recommendations of a new plan funded by the EC, proposed by the Ministry of Tourism. As well as expansion of the industry, the government is hoping for diversification based on better harnessing of the natural attractions of the Maldives. Some islands could be developed as health resorts; the islands are ideal for cruising by yachts and hotel ships; surfing holidays could be developed in a professional way.

"We cannot afford to look at the short term," said the Minister. "Actually, we are sacrificing a lot by not doing so. We could easily expand since the demand is there. But we don't want to ruin the industry. Numbers don't matter."

At present, less than 6% of the nation's uninhabited islands have been developed for tourism. While a few more will also become developed, the vast majority of some 90% will remain as they are, preserved as a kind of green belt of deserted, coral islands.

"We want sustainable development and an industry that will be of benefit for generations to come," said the Minister.

Another principle in the support of the government for tourism is the encouragement the industry can give to Maldivians, not only to finding fulfilling employment in resorts, but also to invest in and even operate resorts. While foreign investors may have access to greater funding, the Maldivian entrepreneur has a special understanding of the industry.

"Single-owner operations offer tourists something unique," said the Minister, referring to individuals who own only one island which they manage with innovative flair. "We are keen, too, to see small-scale industries, such as handicrafts, to be developed as support to resort operators. We would like an equitable distribution of wealth from the tourist industry."

Since the income from tourism circulates very quickly into the economy of the host country, the opportunities for Maldivians to benefit by opening their own successful businesses serving the industry are considerable. Now that the industry has matured, the offspring can share in the celebration too.

The Jubilee Years

In 1965, the Maldives joined the UN and international experts in various fields began to visit the islands. In 1966 an expert arrived to report on the viability of the UN's new member. The expert considered the situation at the time and decided quite definitely that there was no future in tourism for the Maldives.

While the expert was clearly a failure as a fortune-teller, his conclusion was not surprising given the state of the Maldives in the mid 1960s. The airport was a makeshift runway which had recently replaced the one of slotted steel sheets laid out by the British Royal Air Force. Male' resembled a village, a combination of streets of sand, thatched huts, coral cottages and dull administration buildings. Communication with the outside world was by morse code and ham radio. Travel between the islands was by sailing *dhoni*.

The expert must have been appalled. Even if the virgin beaches had won his bureaucratic heart, he would have asked—quite rightly—where is the infrastructure

to support international tourism? There was no proper airport, no source of food beyond fish, no inter-island transport and, as far as he could see, no local funds to develop tourism. There was not even a bank. Since everything tourists would require would have to be imported, tourism hardly seemed an industry that would succeed, let alone help the Maldives to prosper.

So the Maldives remained undisturbed—and unfunded for tourism development —as other experts came and went. Progress did trickle in, but slower than a sailing *dhoni* becalmed at sea. In 1971 there was a great surge forward to the future: a radio telephone link was established between the Maldives and the country's high commission in Colombo.

Adventurous travellers, however, did manage to find their way to the Maldives. Since such visitors were romantic dreamers, not bureaucrats, the potential of the islands for a restful, natural holiday experience was obvious to them.

One such visitor in 1971 was George Corbin, an Italian. He realised he had stumbled on the perfect holiday destination. The fact that there was nowhere to stay and no reliable way to fly in was a problem. It would have to be solved with government and private sector help, and outside involvement and promotion. Corbin's enthusiasm was shared by several Maldivians. So he arranged to return to Male' with a group of people who would publicise the Maldives and attract tourists.

Early in 1972 a group of guests, most of them connected with the travel industry in Italy, flew into the Hulule airstrip from Colombo on a plane chartered from Air Ceylon. They stayed in three private houses in Male' and were looked after by some young Maldivians, including Mohamed Umar Maniku.

"We took them to a different island every day," M.U. Maniku has said. "We didn't know what to cook for them, or how to deal with them."

A colleague of his has recalled those days. "As a group of friends we were accustomed to going to uninhabited islands near Male' to spend a day or two camping, swimming, fishing and barbecuing what we caught to eat on the beach. We didn't know then that we were actually 'domestic tourists'. It gave us the idea of how to entertain these foreign tourists. We just hoped they would enjoy what we enjoyed, and, of course, they did."

Corbin's group of 22 stayed ten days and everyone of them liked what they saw. As long as air access could be improved and some basic accommodation provided on the islands, they believed tourists would adore the Maldives too.

Several Maldivians have been recognised for the part they played in helping start the tourist industry. As well as M.U. Maniku (now chairman of Universal Enterprises) there was Ahmed Naseem (Phoenix Travels) who was a partner with him in MUMAN, a travel agency. There was also Champa Hussein Afeef of the Crown Company, Kandi Ahmed Ismail Manik of Embudhu Village, Ahmed Adam and Saleema Mohamed Kaleyfaan of Phoenix Travels.

In May 1972 the government entered into an agreement with Air Ceylon for the operation of scheduled air services between the Maldives and Sri Lanka. The access problem was partially solved by this, as long as the tourists could get to Sri Lanka.

M. U. Maniku tackled the problem of accommodation by leasing the island of Vihamanaafushi (now Kurumba) which was near both the airport and Male'. Thirty cabanas, each with a makeshift bathroom, were built of coconut wood and palm thatch. The resort opened in October 1972. At the same time, a company called Crescent Tourist Agency with the then president, Ibrahim Nasir, as a major shareholder began a similar operation in Bandos, which opened a few weeks later.

The tourism industry had begun. Any doubts that visitors would be put off by the rustic style of accommodation were quickly dispelled. They loved it.

Statistics record a total of 266 visitors to the Maldives in December 1972, by which time there were 60 beds in Kurumba and 220 in Bandos. In December of the following year, there were 1,069 visitors and four more island resorts had opened: Baros (with 56 beds), Villingili (now reconverted as a residential island) with 208 beds, Furana (now Full Moon) with 112 beds, and Farukolhufushi (now Club Med) with 112 beds. Visitors in 1972 totalled 1,097; then increased by 245.5% to 3,790 in 1973.

Despite its obvious potential being confirmed by the first tourists, the finding of financing for the industry was difficult. The first bank did not open until 1974. Although many of the Maldivian entrepreneurs had close links with Sri Lanka, their Sri Lankan friends looked askance at the idea of investing in tourism in the Maldives.

"We had to pay highly in commissions to Sri Lankan travel agents," M.U. Maniku has said. "Yet we needed every cent we could make, so it could be reinvested to improve the facilities, and build new resorts."

Rooms were contracted to tour operators and the advance payments helped to finance the building. Credit for supplies could only be obtained from farsighted Singapore exporters which resulted in links being forged which still hold firm today.

Tourism Grows to Order

The first tourists were Italians. They were followed quickly by Scandinavians. Realising the impact that tourism could have on the economy, both the private sector and government did whatever was required to encourage it. When there were comments from tourists about having to go through a lengthy and tiresome immigration and customs inspection under rather primitive conditions at the Hulule airport, it was decided in 1975 to relax procedures.

Tourists arrived and were transferred straight to the resorts with no inspection whatsoever. Some even asked for an entry to be made in their passports by the resort receptionist just to prove that they had been in the Maldives.

By 1976, the number of visitors had risen to 12,477 with October to April being recognised by European tourists as the best time. The influx of tourists resulted in more resorts being built for them (there were 17 by the end of 1978) and in an improvement in communications.

The implications of a flourishing tourism industry were immediately recognised under the new administration of President Gayoom. In October 1979, he appointed Ahmed Mujuthaba, a dedicated technocrat with communications, airline and shipping experience as the first director of the newly created Department of Tourism and Foreign Investment.

A law on tourism which outlines basic regulations for the industry was passed in 1979, in an effort to make tourism both viable and worthwhile to the Maldives. A bed tax (currently US$6.00 per night per person and included in the room rate) was introduced, bringing about a fast and direct contribution to the country on behalf of every visitor. A ten-year tourism plan was commissioned.

In 1981, the airport at Hulule which had expanded gradually to take flights from the subcontinent was officially opened as Male' International Airport. This resulted in travel agents being able to send their clients direct to the Maldives by the charter aircraft of such companies as Condor, LTU and Alitalia. Word of mouth advertising by satisfied guests did the rest to set off the tourism boom.

The regulations brought in during the 1980s defined minimum standards. A survey of resort islands at the time revealed that only about 14% of the land area of each resort was actually utilised for buildings. Preservation of the environmental appeal of a tourist island had been carried out instinctively by resort developers who recognised that visitors wanted as much unspoiled natural beauty as possible.

The latest trend of building rooms as cabanas on stilts, or apartments on pillars, in an island's lagoon has not led to overcrowding. This is because of the rule that, for every room built on pillars over a lagoon, equal space should be left free on the island.

FACING PAGE
A dhoni sails past Kudabandos, an uninhabited island near Male' in Kaafu Atoll. Kaafu Atoll (inset map) is the main tourist resort area of the Maldives.

GEGENÜBERLIEGENDE SEITE
Ein Dhoni segelt an Kudabandos, einer unbewohnten Insel nahe Male im Kaafu-Atoll, vorüber. Das Kaafu-Atoll (eingefügte Karte) ist das größte Feriengebiet für Touristen auf den Malediven.

PAGINA A FRONTE
Una dhoni passa di fronte a Kudabandos, un'isola disabitata vicino a Malè nell'atollo di Kaafu. L'atollo Kaafu (vedi la mappa) è la principale area turistica delle Maldive.

KAAFU
ATOLL

INDIAN
OCEAN

• Gafaru

• Helengeli

Eriyadhu •

Makunudo •

Summer Island
Village •
Reethi Rah •
(Medhufinolhu)

Hembadhoo •

Asdu •
• Meerufenfushi
Dhiffushi

Boduhiti •
Kudahiti •

Thulusdhu
Lhohifushi • • Gasfinolhu
Nakatchafushi •
Hura • Kanifinolhu
• Kuda Hura Reef Resort
Tari Village •

Thulagiri •
Ihuru •
Banyan Tree •
Himmafushi
• Hudhuveli
Paradise •

Baros •
• Bandos
• Full Moon

Kurumba •
• Farukolhufushi
(Club Med)

INDIAN

OCEAN

• Giraavaru
✈ • International Airport

Villingili □
MALE'

Laguna Beach • Vadoo •
• Embudhu Finolhu
Bolifushi •
• Embudhu Village

Gulhi

Dhigufinolhu •
• Veligandu Huraa
(Palm Tree)

Mafushi

Biyadoo •
Viliivaru • • Cocoa Island
Club Rannalhi • • Kadooma
Guraidhu

Fihalhohi •

• Fun Island
• Olhuveli View

• Rihiveli

N

KEY
• Inhabited Island
• Tourist Resort

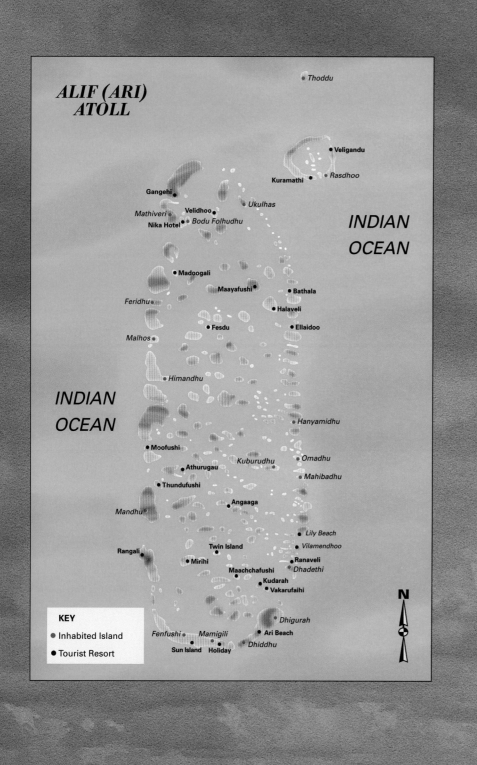

ALIF (ARI)
ATOLL

Thoddu

Veligandu

Kuramathi • Rasdhoo

Gangehi

Ukulhas

INDIAN
OCEAN

Mathiveri • Velidhoo
Nika Hotel • Bodu Folhudhu

Madoogali

Maayafushi • Bathala

Feridhu • Halaveli

Fesdu • Ellaidoo

Malhos

Himandhu

INDIAN
OCEAN

Hanyamidhu

Moofushi

Kuburudhu • Omadhu

Athurugau • Mahibadhu

Thundufushi

Angaaga

Lily Beach

Twin Island • Vilamendhoo

Rangali • Ranaveli

Mirihi • Dhadethi
Maachchafushi
Kudarah
Vakarufaihi

N

Dhigurah

KEY
• Inhabited Island
• Tourist Resort

Fenfushi • Mamigili • Ari Beach
Sun Island   Holiday • Dhiddhu

Tourism Expands

Apart from the exceptions of Alimatha in Vaavu Atoll which opened in 1975, Kuramathi, north of Ari Atoll, which started in 1977, and Kuredhdhu (1978) in far-off Lhaviyani Atoll, all resorts were in North or South Male' Atoll. The first resorts to open in Ari Atoll, which now has 26 resort islands, were Fesdu and Halaveli, in 1982.

The real development of Ari Atoll followed the commissioning of Ari Atoll Tourism Zone in 1988. The resorts were developed then by the private sector who concentrated on supplying for themselves all the services and infrastructure they needed.

At the end of 1975, there were 908 beds in eight resorts. By 1985, there were 55 resorts with 5,375 beds. By the end of 1995, 73 resorts accounted for 10,688 beds.

The statistics do not reveal what was actually happening on each resort island: the thatched cabanas with sand floors and wooden shutters for windows, with brackish water in the bathroom, were being replaced. Having captured a section of the tourist business for the Maldives, resort operators were determined not to lose it by complacency.

"Tourists built the industry here," M.U. Maniku has said. "We listened to them and gave them what they wanted."

Of course, visitors from different backgrounds wanted different holiday environments. While the European market preferred designer rustic—back to nature with a touch of sophistication—Asian visitors looked for city amenities, like television and airconditioning, in their tropical islands.

Because of their understanding of visitor requirements and due to the success of their first ventures, the tourism pioneers were able to create resorts that cater for all tastes, from Grand Hotel extravagant luxury to beachcomber simplicity. Each resort has its own image, appealing to a particular kind of guest, who soon grows to love it for a holiday. Over 20% of tourists are regular repeat visitors.

Even while tourism is enjoying a boom and there are not always enough beds to go round, resort operators know the industry is a fragile one. Research has shown that guests are satisfied with the infrastructure and the choice of resorts. To maintain momentum the aim is to improve on the extras and on the quality of hospitality.

"Maldivians are shy, modest people," one resort manager has said. "We have to be more extrovert with our guests, letting them see how welcome they are."

It is a welcome more guests are discovering each year. Current arrivals are increasing by 15% every 12 months. Now the resorts are fully booked for most months each year.

It is a state of affairs no one would have dreamed of 25 years ago, so perhaps the expert could be forgiven for his hopelessly inaccurate prediction.

FACING PAGE
Uninhabited islands, such as this, have been turned into resorts in Alif (Ari) Atoll and are the natural resource sustaining responsible tourism development.

GEGENÜBERLIEGENDE SEITE
Unbewohnte Inseln, wie diese, sind im Alif- (Ari-) Atoll touristisch erschlossen worden und bieten die natürlichen Resourcen für eine verantwortungsbewußte Entwicklung des Tourismus.

PAGINA A FRONTE
Isole disabitate, come questa, sono state trasformate in località turistiche negli atolli Alif (Ari) e sono le risorse naturali che sostengono uno sviluppo consapevole del turismo.

The Complete Holiday: Have a Nice Stay

The Ultimate Resort

Every resort island has its individual image. While a small resort that is the favourite of a visitor from Europe may not appeal to a tourist from Asia, major resorts with many activities manage to provide an agreeable welcome for all nationalities.

A typical resort island will have the basics of a sandy beach and a lagoon safe for bathing and snorkelling. Some have house reefs ideal for diving just a few metres off shore. From others, the best diving is a few minutes away by *dhoni*.

Accommodation will range from rooms with *sataa* (woven screw pine) ceilings and rustic fittings to the luxuries of a modern airconditioned city-style apartment, or from log cabins built over the lagoon to duplexes in the wilderness. A separate bathroom (with bath and/or shower with hot water, and toilet) will be en suite with every guestroom. At some resorts the bathroom will have its own walled garden open to the sky in imitation of the Maldivian village *gifili* (bathroom).

All resorts have at least one restaurant, with meals included in the room rate; many resorts also have another area where à la carte meals are available. Some resorts provide a holiday that really is "all inclusive"—not only meals but drinks and even cigarettes are included in the room rate as well as leisure activities like watersports and a visit to a fishing village island.

Luxury resorts offer a choice of as many as six restaurants. All resorts would be willing to handle special requests such as a candlelight dinner on the beach. There will be a bar open until the last guest leaves; some resorts also have minibars in their rooms. While the atmosphere will be gloriously informal in some resorts with sand on the floor of the restaurant as well as on the beach, others have staff in bow ties and airconditioned restaurants where guests are served in five-star style.

The only diversion in the evening in some resorts will be watching the sunset and the spread of heavenly colours across the sky. Others will offer a pop music band from Male' and karaoke.

On some islands your postcards home will be mailed when a *dhoni* goes to Male', on others an efficient business centre and reception staff will make you want to

FACING AND FOLLOWING PAGES
Guests relax in the beach garden of a resort island while thatched log cabins above a lagoon offer the luxurious accommodation castaways dream of.

GEGENÜBERLIEGENDE UND FOLGENDE SEITEN
Gäste entspannen sich im Garten am Strand einer Hotelinsel; strohgedeckte Blockhütten oberhalb der Lagune bieten luxuriöse Unterkünfte, von denen Fernwehkranke träumen.

PAGINA DI FRONTE E PAGINE SEGUENTI
Turisti si rilassano nel giardino sulla spiaggia di un'isola; capanne coperte da tegole lignee sulla lagune offrono sistemazioni di sogno.

relocate your own office there. Some islands have convention centres and host international conferences, others offer guests an entire island for the day for a private tête à tête. There are resorts ideal for honeymooners and others more suited to the diving enthusiast.

All resorts have an adequate supply of fresh water from desalinisation plants, backed up by rainwater catchments. All have their own electricity generators. Disposal of waste is planned, not haphazard.

All islands have a diving school with a trained instructor who supervises diving for beginners and experienced divers. All islands have some watersports like windsurfing and beach or ball games arranged between staff and guests. Only a few islands have animators since resort management have found that guests prefer to enjoy themselves in their own fashion.

Staff on the resorts will be of many nationalities but those whom guests encounter most, in the restaurants or on boat trips, will be Maldivian. By law, the bartender will be non-Maldivian.

While prices range from US$65 to over $500 for two, full board, the price in a brochure does not give much clue about the character of the resort. There are some resorts where prices are in the upper range because they provide a calculatedly simple ambience, not luxury. On the other hand, a lower priced resort may have all the service and extras one would expect from a five-star hotel.

In some resorts, the commitment to saving the environment means leaving the island as nature intended, with very few flowers or gardeners to tend to the vegetation. Others see enhancement of an island's beauty as a better way of saving the environment and its gardens will be lush with flora and fauna, making a setting that is romantic rather than rustic.

Since guests come from dozens of countries, and from different stratas of society, each has different expectations. The resorts in the Maldives truly cater for everyone. When resort and guest match perfectly, you know you have found the *ultimate* resort.

The Voice of Tourism

The Maldives Association of Tourism Industry (MATI) is a private sector organisation concerned with the quality and vitality of the tourist industry. Its members are resort operators, travel agents, foreign tour operators, airlines, diving schools and entrepreneurs. It was formed in 1979, not just to develop the industry but to do so in a way that ensures the industry in the Maldives has a viable future.

MATI is the industry's voice in dealing with government. Being in touch with the tourist industry worldwide it is able to monitor trends and ensure that the Maldives remains competitive and does not lose its appeal. After 25 years of tourism and the development of resorts to suit every kind of guest, on every kind of budget, MATI sees it as important to emphasise the extras and hospitality of a Maldivian holiday.

MATI does not encourage mass-market tourism, preferring to concentrate on giving good value for money. One way of doing this is through training schemes to make sure each guest gets the best attention. MATI has projected that by 1998 there will be enough Maldivians to fill the staff demands and key positions of the industry. However, at least 12% of the industry's staff must necessarily be expatriates because of the need for foreign bar staff.

Intensive Caring

In many resorts you are likely to meet a young Maldivian at management level who seems especially motivated. He smiles well, speaks articulately, knows his job and seems to care. It is a pleasure to talk with him and to realise that he will do all he can to make your stay memorable. Enquire about his background and you will probably discover he is a graduate of the Institute of Hotel and Catering Services.

The training that students are given at the Institute is tough, a two-year course based on British standards compacted into one year of intensive training. "In the Maldives," explained the Director, "students don't like to study longer; they want to go out into the industry."

In what used to be a government guesthouse at Sosunge in Male', the Institute was founded in 1987 as the School of Hotel and Catering Services.

The curriculum has evolved until it has reached the standard where the course is recognised by British institutions, with a B. Tech diploma awarded to graduates. Training is provided in all departments of hotel management. Even if a student intends to work in food and beverage, he learns about every other aspect to gain an all-round knowledge.

Resorts also organise their own in-house and extramural training schemes for all levels of staff. Some staff are sent abroad on familiarisation programmes so they can learn about the expectations and home country background of their guests, as well as gaining a deeper knowledge of the hospitality industry. Maldivians are no longer isolated in the industry and frequently win medals and recognition at international exhibitions and fairs.

FOLLOWING PAGES
Page 40: There is plenty of "after beach" entertainment at major resorts: Barbecue by the beach (top left); exotic table d'hôte restaurant in a resort island (top right); disco time (bottom left); a nightcap in the bar (bottom right). Page 41: (top) A glass of wine at sunset; (bottom) An antique style bedroom created with a rustic look.

FOLGENDE SEITEN
Seite 40: Große Ferienanlagen bieten vielerlei Unterhaltung nach einem Tag am Strand: Barbecue am Strand (links oben); exotisches Table d'hôte-Restaurant auf einer Hotelinsel (rechts oben); Discovergnügen (links unten); Schlummertrunk in der Bar (rechts unten); Seite 41: (oben) ein Glas Wein bei Sonnenuntergang; (unten) ein Schlafzimmer im altmodischen Stil mit ruraler Atmosphäre.

PAGINE SEQUENTI
Pagina 40: Ci sono molti intrattenimenti "dopo-spiaggia" nei villaggi principali: Barbecue sulla spiaggia (a sinistra in alto); esotica tavola di ristorante (sopra, a destra); discoteca (sotto, a sinistra); l'ultimo bicchiere al bar prima di dormire (sotto, a destra). Pagina 41: (sopra) un bicchiere di vino al tramonto; (sotto) una camera da letto in stile antico disegnata in stile rustico.

Gateway to Paradise

If you had a chance to look out of your window as your jet circled low over the Maldives, you probably wondered where it was going to land. It looks as though the jet is landing on the sea as it touches down on a runway extending into the shimmering blue waters of a lagoon.

The sight of sun-soaked beaches and the embrace of warmth that greets passengers, quickly sets the holiday mood. But don't dash off to swim yet (as one eager tourist once did, throwing her clothes off as she streaked across the tarmac to the beach.) There is another journey to take to your resort from the airport island.

With a new arrival and departure terminal that opened in May 1996, the airport building is one of the most modern and pleasant in the region. The processing of arriving passengers is brief and takes place in a long, well-lit and airconditioned hall. All nationalities are given a 30-day permit at the immigration desk.

There are lots of trolleys for transporting luggage from the conveyor belts to customs. There, suitcases are usually X-rayed instead of opened and searched. Questions might be asked to make sure you have nothing (like alcohol, pork products or risqué pictures) that could cause offence to Maldivians. Drugs are, of course, prohibited.

There is a tourist information counter on the right of the exit door. Outside representatives are waiting to greet their clients and escort them to the jetty, or to check-in desk for helicopter or seaplane transfer to the resorts.

The departure process is bound to be sad after an enjoyable holiday, but the airport makes the experience stress-free. There are plenty of places to sit and wait in the sun (or shade) until the last moment. Last minute purchases can be made at the souvenir shop and the post shop outside the terminal. Inside, after checking in, there is a surprise as you enter the familiar world of a high-class shopping mall.

There are duty-free shops selling the latest in fashions and fragrancies, liquor, confectionary and gifts. In a store artistically designed like a forest, the range of liquor on sale is staggering, from inexpensive brands to premium products, on shelves that look like part of a tree. The confectionery shop has caviar, gourmet items, chocolate and local goodies like breadfruit chips and whole coconuts. You can buy cameras, watches and electronics, prestige fountain pens and exquisite jewellery and computer toys. For many visitors, the quality of the duty-free shopping, at prices to suit all budgets, may seem a surprise after the simple island life, but it proves that the Maldives has everything.

Opposite the duty-free shopping mall are the departure lounges and a restaurant, all with views of the runway. The Finifenmaa Lounge run by Air Maldives is available for use by VIPs and airline premium class passengers.

The airport and its buildings have grown with tourism. Not just the travelling public gains, but the quality of life of people who never leave their islands is improved, since the airport enables swift handling of perishable items and all other freight.

FACING PAGE

Top left and top right: An Air Maldives Dornier propeller aircraft flies over the islets of the Maldives and a pilot's view of Male' International Airport. Bottom left (top and below): Checking by customs at the airport is swift and friendly while duty free shops at the airport provide quality shopping on departure. Centre right and bottom right: A seaplane service operates to resorts and village islands with dhonis *providing the necessary transfers to the destinations.*

GEGENÜBERLIEGENDE SEITE

Oben links und rechts: Eine Dornier-Maschine der örtlichen Fluggesellschaft Air Maldives überfliegt die kleinen Malediven-Inseln, und Males internationaler Flughafen aus der Vogelflugperspektive. Links unten (oben und darunter): Reisende werden beim Zoll am Flughafen schnell und mit freundlichem Lächeln abgefertigt; Duty-free Geschäfte am Fughafen bieten erstklassige Einkaufsmöglichkeiten vor dem Abflug. Mitte rechts und unten rechts: Wasserflugzeuge fliegen zu den Ferienanlagen und den Dörfern der Inseln, auch Dhonis *bringen Besucher zu ihrem Reiseziel.*

PAGINA A FRONTE

Sopra a sinistra e a destra: Un velivolo a elica Dormier della linea aerea delle Maldive sorvola le isole, e la vista che un pilota gode dell'aeroporto internazionale di Malè. Sotto a sinistra (sopra e sotto): Il passaggio attraverso la dogana all'aeroporto è scorrevole ed amichevole, ed i negozi duty free all'aeroporto sono forniti di articoli interessanti da acquistare prima della partenza. Al centro, destra e sotto, destra: un acquaplano effettua servizio verso villaggi turistici e le dhonis *provvedono ai necessari trasferimenti nelle rispettive destinazioni.*

The Nation's Airline

Air Maldives, the nation's airline, has its origins in the same year that tourism began. In May 1972, the government entered into an agreement with Air Ceylon to operate bi-monthly flights using Avros and Heron Riley aircraft of the Sri Lanka Air Force.

The service was endearingly informal. An employee at the time recalls that passengers, as well as their luggage, had to be weighed before boarding. The Heron Riley aircraft was rather old and could not take off if it was overloaded. So passengers weighing a lot were given the privilege of flying on the newer Avros, while the thin ones were sent skywards to Sri Lanka on the Herons.

Since tourists demanded more efficient air access, Air Maldives was set up in 1974, using leased aircraft to provide a more frequent service. Various associations with other airlines and operating refinements eventually led, in 1994, to the setting up of Air Maldives Ltd. The airline has an international network stretching from Dubai to Kuala Lumpur, via Maldives. It also provides a gateway service by its Airbus 300, from Trivandrum.

Air Maldives in association with the Maldives Airports Authority acts as the ground handling agent for all the foreign airlines serving the Maldives. On domestic routes Dornier D0228 propeller aircraft, seating 18 passengers, serve four atoll airports: Gan, Kadhdhoo, Hanimadhoo and Kaadedhoo. Air links to the atolls were further improved with the setting up of two helicopter companies that operate to helipads near resort islands and a seaplane service that operates to resort islands, and anywhere in the Maldives on special charter.

All at Sea

For most, the dream of a visit to the Maldives becomes real with the transfer from the airport to the resort. If this is by air there is the breathtaking views of beach-girt islands set in turquoise lagoons, causing one to reflect at several hundred metres up, on the phenomenal beauty of creation.

Those in less of a rush, prefer the poetry of motion in travelling by sea. While speedboats will get you to the holiday island in a hurry, the real rhythm of the islands is best experienced by slow *dhoni* at sea level.

The gentle beat of the motor as the boat glides across azure seas allows you to adjust gradually to this new, leisurely pace. What seemed so important when you left home wafts away with the caress of the sea breeze. The urgency of time no longer applies to you now that sunrise and sunset structure the Maldivian day.

The transfer by *dhoni* to an island resort is a chance to realise how Maldivians depend on the sea, not only for food but also for their links with other islands. The sea does not divide them but provides the highway from one island to another.

At times, of course, it can be an uncompromising, demanding friend. That happens during the southwest monsoon period when seas are rough. Since the monsoon brings much needed rain, it is welcomed. Usually, though, the transfer from and back to the airport is an enjoyable extra, a pleasant sea cruise.

Motorised *dhonis* serve islands close to the airport while speedboats, and some small high-powered cruising craft, provide transfer to islands further away. There are no ferry boats that ply between islands to a schedule. Most journeys between resorts, even those in the same atoll, have to be done on boats travelling via the airport island, or Male', unless you charter your own.

Island Cruising

Island hopping by *dhoni* from one island to another has developed, in response to demands by visitors for a way to see more of the Maldives, into a well-organised experience: the diving safari cruise.

Typical accommodation on a safari boat includes a dining room, a galley with a cook adept at preparing dishes of fish freshly caught by passengers and crew, a sundeck and cabins. Some have cabins for two with bunks, or a large common cabin with pairs of bunks separated by curtains. All boats have toilets (flushed with sea water) and at least one freshwater shower. They are equipped with a refrigerator, generator, CB radio and a dinghy with outboard motor.

Most passengers go on a safari cruise as a way to visit unspoiled dive locations and to voyage gently in atolls instead of staying at one resort for the whole of their holiday. Safari cruises take place in atolls where there are facilities for tourists, mainly in Male' and Ari atolls. The vessels anchor each night and guests can go ashore to visit a resort, but they sleep on board.

The safari cruise concept has, like the tourism industry itself, matured to offer a better holiday. Safari cruising has evolved to include what are virtually small passenger cruise liners designed solely for leisurely voyaging between the atolls.

The *Atoll Explorer* was the first such ship. It has 20 double cabins, each with large windows and, in some cabins, private balconies. All have a freshwater shower and a toilet en suite. Cabins are airconditioned. The atmosphere on board is that of an exclusive, well-run, floating family hotel.

There is a saloon with a cocktail bar and an open-sided deck restaurant where the food rivals that of the resorts in quality and variety. There is ample space to lie in the sun, and there are even two jacuzzi whirlpool tubs on deck for passengers to wallow in luxury. There are also facilities for divers with a dive school on board.

With its unpolluted waters and pristine beaches, the Maldives is the substance of holiday dreams.

BELOW AND FACING PAGE
Cruising in comfort. A cabin on the Atoll Explorer has all the comforts of home while a fruit basket is delivered for guests on a safari boat.

UNTEN UND GEGENÜBERLIEGENDE SEITE
Eine Kreuzfahrt mit allem Komfort. Eine Kabine auf der Atoll Explorer bietet allen Komfort, den der Besucher von zuhause gewöhnt ist; ein Korb mit Früchten wird den Gästen auf einem Ausflugsboot gebracht.

SOTTO E PAGINA A FRONTE
Navigando in comodità. Una cabina dell'Atoll Explorer ha tutti i comforts di una casa, mentre un cesto di frutta viene recapitato ai turisti su un'imbarcazione da safari.

The Smile of Faith

The Influence of Islam

The smile of the Maldivian is shy and respectful. It is not a swift bestowal of an unfeeling blessing, but a reflection of a deep and genuine delight at a shared emotion. When a smile seems slow to dawn on the face of a Maldivian casually met, it is a sign of assessment, not disapproval.

Visitors accustomed to the flashing grin of a sudden acquaintance or of people who have something, even friendship, to sell, will look in vain for a similar soulless smile in the Maldives. The Maldivian smile is born of the warmth and hospitality of independent islanders bolstered by their unswerving faith.

The inner strength imparted by the islanders' collective belief in Islam is apparent in every encounter. There is none of the stridence of grasping, competitive societies. Disagreements, when they occur, are settled peaceably; revenge does not linger in the Maldivian breast.

When a Maldivian feels wronged, he will retain his dignity and adjust his life accordingly. Living in the Maldives, where no man is an island, has created a powerful people who know that sharing is the only means of survival, and that all are family, according to the tenets of their religion.

Islam plays a dominant role in every Maldivian's life, even for those living in the smallest, remotest island. Every inhabited island has at least one mosque. There is also a mosque on each of the resort islands, so even when Maldivians are caught up in the glamour of the holiday mood, they can repair to the mosque for familiar solace.

The religion of Maldivians is not the demanding faith it may seem to visitors. Being brought up within Islam's embrace is a gentle, submissive experience that moulds a personality attune to both the hardships and rewards of island living. In Male', where sophistication abounds, Islam is just as strong as in the isolated islands; worship at a mosque remains a crucial part of everyday life in the capital.

The call to prayer sings out five times a day; it is reassurance that all is well, not solely to summon all to the mosque. Women worship privately in separate mosques or in defined sections of a shared mosque. The Islamic faith of Maldivians is exclusively the tolerant Sunni Muslim kind, which is why the development of tourism has been permitted in tandem with the rule of religion.

FACING PAGE
Every inhabited island has a mosque where children as well as adults worship.

GEGENÜBERLIEGENDE SEITE
Auf jeder bewohnten Insel findet sich eine Moschee, in der sowohl Kinder als auch Erwachsene beten.

PAGINA A FRONTE
Ogni isola abitata ha una moschea, meta di preghiera per adulti e bambini.

The President's Role

With Islam the religion of the State and the backbone of society, the President of the Maldives is the supreme authority entrusted with its protection. In the person of the present president, His Excellency Maumoon Abdul Gayoom, the Maldives has a leader qualified intellectually as well as spiritually for the task.

President Gayoom holds a Bachelor of Arts degree in Islamic Studies, awarded in 1964, for which he studied at the Al Azhar University in Cairo, Egypt. He also holds a Diploma of Education awarded by the same university in 1965 and is a Master of Arts in Islamic Studies, awarded in 1966.

President Gayoom was selected by the Citizens' Majlis as the presidential candidate for the national referendum held in November 1978 when he polled 92.9% of the votes. He became President for a five-year term, replacing the incumbent, Ibrahim Nasir, who had been President for 10 years.

President Gayoom was returned to office by referendum for a fourth term in November 1993.

Born in Male' in 1937, His Excellency Maumoom Abdul Gayoom was educated in Male' and in the then Ceylon for a short period of time before going to Egypt for further studies. He married the First Lady, Nasreena Ibrahim, while in Egypt and is the father of twin daughters and two sons. He intended to pursue an academic career and became Research Assistant to the Professor of Islamic History at the American University of Cairo from 1967 to 1969 followed by a two-year period, 1969 to 1971, as lecturer in Islamic Studies and Philosophy at Abdullahi Bayero College of Ahmadu Bello University, Nigeria.

He returned to the Maldives in 1971 and became a teacher at the Aminiya School in Male'. His teaching career was interrupted by banishment to an island for supposed political activity and he later served a period of 50 days in jail while under investigation for political involvement.

The President was manager of the Shipping Department, 1972-1973 and, briefly, Under Secretary, Telecommunications Department, and Director, Telephone Department, in 1974.

He was Special Under Secretary in the Office of the Prime Minister, 1974-1975, before becoming Deputy Ambassador of the Maldives in Sri Lanka in 1975-1976. He served as Under Secretary in the Department of External Affairs, and Deputy Minister of Transport, in 1976, and then became the Permanent Representative of the Maldives to the United Nations, September 1976 to March 1977. He was re-called to Male' to become the country's Minister of Transport in March 1977, a post he held until the assumption of office as President.

President Maumoon Abdul Gayoom is also Commander-in-Chief of the Armed Forces and the Minister of Defence and National Security, as well as Minister of Finance and Treasury, and Governor of the Maldives Monetary Authority.

Tourism: A Presidential View

With a background of academia and the discipline of religion as well as of administration and the shifting sands of politics, Maumoom Abdul Gayoom has brought rare qualities to the post of President. He is devoutly dedicated to his country and also shows a professorial-like concern for the cares of his people. He is as understanding of people's foibles as he is appreciative of their strengths.

In an interview granted especially for *A Maldives Celebration*, he answered the following questions:

Q. *What are your personal recollections of the Maldives in the 1970s when tourism began?*

A. Things were very different then. Living standards were much lower. There were no high-rise buildings in Male'. No TV, no mechanised *dhonis* and very few cars. The only important economic activity was fishing. Job opportunities were few. Schools were centred in Male'. But, there were some positive aspects too. As the population was small, the country as a whole, and Male' in particular, was very clean and free of environmental pollution. When tourism began, the Maldives opened up for the outside world, and the pace of economic and social growth increased tremendously.

Q. *How did you view the potential benefits to the Maldives from tourism when you were first elected president?*

A. A lot of us used to think about the potential of tourism in the Maldives even in the days when we were studying in Egypt in the 1960s. Tourism was already flourishing in Egypt then, and we were sure that tourism would be of immense benefit to the Maldives too. When I was first elected President in 1978, there were only 17 tourist resorts then with a total of 1,300 beds. I was convinced that tourism could provide a major breakthrough for our economic development. Consequently, we have invested heavily in tourism and have tried very hard to promote the Maldives as an attractive destination.

Q. *Did you have any misgivings, and what was the eventual outcome if you did have misgivings?*

A. "Misgiving" is a rather strong word. So I won't say I had any misgivings. But as you would agree, when entering into an entirely new venture with so many unknown factors involved, it is only natural that there would be some doubts as to its long-terms benefits. More so because most of the tourists were coming from countries with a totally different cultural background. I too wondered at the beginning what effects the growth of tourism would have on our society. Fortunately, we have been able to develop tourism here in a way that had no negative impacts on our social and cultural values. In fact, the benefits that we are getting from tourism far outweigh any ill effects it may have had on our society.

Q. *What changes did you introduce to set tourism on a course that would bring maximum benefit to the Maldives and all Maldivians?*

A. We introduced the concept of "planned tourism" to bring in maximum benefits. The first ten-year tourism master plan came into force in 1983. It was aimed at ensuring sustainability, a positive impact on the environment, and giving more incentives to the private sector. After the successful completion of that plan, we have now embarked on the second ten-year tourism master plan which is targeted towards the sustainable development of this sector and the spread of its benefits to a much wider area of the country. We have also institutionalised the leasing of uninhabited islands for tourism development through legislation. Undoubtedly, all Maldivians directly or indirectly have benefited from the relative prosperity generated by tourism.

Q. *What are your feeling about the state of tourism today?*

A. I am very happy about the growth of tourism in the Maldives. We have achieved around 16% annual growth during the past two years. Tourist arrivals increased from

279,982 in 1994 to 314,869 in 1995. The revenue earned increased from Rf 307.8 million to Rf 372 million in that period. It amounts to about 18.4% of our GDP. It is important that we try to upgrade the standard of service at the tourist resorts and hotels, and be more competitive with other destinations.

Q. *Since over 300,000 people from abroad now visit the Maldives on holiday every year, what impression of the Maldives would you like those people to take back with them?*

A. That of the peace and stability prevailing in our country, as well as that of our unique culture and way of life. In addition, that of both the beauty and the fragility of our ecosystem.

Q. *How can people who enjoy the Maldives for a holiday contribute to maintaining and improving the quality of life for all Maldivians?*

A. Tourism is the No. 1 foreign exchange earner of the Maldives. The revenue generated is fully utilised towards further social and economic progress. Individual tourists too could contribute to our quality of life if they appreciate the natural beauty of the islands and the surrounding marine environment and help us preserve it the way it is.

Q. *You have spoken internationally about the consequences of rising sea level and its connection with environmental changes caused by industrial progress; in other words the Maldives could suffer because of the developing world. What is being done about this, and what would you like to see done?*

A. Domestically, we are taking all possible measures to protect the environment. A law on the protection and preservation of the environment is in force. A national plan of action is being implemented. Coral mining from house reefs is banned. Tariffs on imported building materials are reduced. Dumping of toxic waste is prohibited, and garbage disposal standards are tightened. Environmental impact assessment of all development projects is required before implementation. Though we are doing all that, it will by no means be enough to protect our country from the threat of sea level rise and other environmental dangers. As you know, the industrialised nations are largely responsible for causing those problems on a global basis. Therefore, it is

the moral responsibility of those countries to do everything possible to save the world from the impending, environmental catastrophe.

Q. *How would you describe to a stranger, in general terms, the average Maldivian?*

A. I would say that the average Maldivian is intelligent, friendly, hardworking and eager to learn.

Q. *What advice would you give to the first-time visitor who comes to the Maldives on holiday?*

A. My advice would be to appreciate and respect our culture and our laws and customs which could be very different from their own, and enjoy the serene beauty of our islands. I would like them also to be conscious of the ecological vulnerability of our islands and avoid causing any harm to our reefs, beaches and other ecosystems.

Q. *What misconceptions in foreigners' minds about the Maldives would you like to see corrected?*

A. I don't know of any serious misconceptions. But, since we are a closely-knit homogeneous society with one faith as the moral and spiritual force that binds us together, there could be certain misconceptions in foreigners' minds about our political and social order. We are certainly a democratic country. Civil liberties and human rights are ensured by our laws. Free and fair elections for the presidency and for parliament are held once every five years. We enjoy a higher degree of political stability and social harmony than in many countries of the region, and indeed, of the world.

Q. *People think that to live on an island is to get away from it all, to escape. Would you agree that life on an island is not an escape, but a hard way of facing up to reality? Perhaps Maldivians are really more in touch with what life is all about than the people of so-called developed countries?*

A. It certainly is not an escape. Our islands are small, with limited resources. Living on such islands is fraught with many hardships. But our people have over the centuries mastered the art of living in such conditions as is evident from the way that they have created a unique culture of their own. Indeed, the average Maldivian living in the far-flung islands leads a relatively happy and relaxed life.

The Dignity of Theemuge

It stands in classical splendour, its clean cut lines defined by the dignified blue of its eaves and balcony edges; it is a graceful edifice of white, serene under a cobalt blue sky in a paved courtyard thronged with flowering plants. This building in Orchid Magu which is the cynosure of all who pass it, is Theemuge, the Presidential Palace.

On the day of Eid-al-Fitr each year, the palace is open for the citizens of the Maldives to greet their President. Visitors who stroll along Orchid Magu where it leads off the Jumhooree Maidan are enchanted by close-up views of where the President lives. Male', being small, has no space for grand buildings that are secluded far from the public's gaze, and Theemuge is no exception. Many visitors photograph the palace through the wrought-iron gates and it is a building whose exterior is worthy of photographic record.

A portico with two pairs of broad, fluted columns on either side supporting its canopy, forms the palace's main entrance. On each side are glass doors and windows with elegant teak frames and antique-style wooden sunrise fanlights, backed by curtains of deep blue. These are fronted by Queen Anne-type wrought-iron blue painted balcony railings. The first floor has external balustraded platforms, each with access doors from upstairs rooms, matching the bold lines of the portico roof.

The facade of the apex that soars above the roof is embossed with the emblematic five-pointed star of the President of the Maldives, dressed in wedgewood blue, distinguishing the palace's style.

The steps up to the entrance door are of light grey mottled marble. The entrance hall and all the reception rooms have marble floors of mottled white and grey, and deep royal green. They are set with traditional Islamic motifs, a theme which is continued in the inlaid wood tracery around the door frame of each carved teak door. The effect is both opulent and tranquil, an impact of colour and light that creates an impression of formality that is stimulating rather than intimidating.

The vaulted recesses set into the walls of the entrance hall have arches of traditional Arabic shape and contain tall lacquered vases on proud display. More lacquer vases stand on scrolled ledges above eye height, an inspired touch of refinement that blends well with the decor and is especially relevant since the vases were made in the Maldives.

On the left of the entrance hall is the waiting saloon, continuing the theme of marble floor set with Islamic emblems, and marble half-panelling on the walls. The decor is subdued but plush. The black model of a fishing *dhoni* on display inevitably forms a talking point for the waiting visitors.

Across the lobby is the reception room used by the First Lady, Madam Nasreena Gayoom, to receive the spouses of visiting dignitaries. Its balcony overlooks the main courtyard. Cabinets contain local handicrafts, including exquisite arrangements of flowers made out of shells.

The main reception hall opens from the entrance lobby. A chandelier hangs from the high ceiling and etched glass panels flood the room with light. A wide staircase leads to private rooms on the first floor with a gallery overlooking the hall, defining the durbar-like atrium where visiting heads of state are received.

The central square of the atrium has marbled columns of mottled green at each of its four corners. Carved wooden friezes, reflecting the transoms of the doorways, are set as decoration into the walls of the overhead gallery. The corners of the gallery are masked by cascades of ivy smothering the crown of each column.

Hanging neatly against wall panels dedicated to pictures, are paintings by Maldivian artists, including a striking one of a simple and wise man, signed "Dunya, 91". It is by the President's daughter.

Doors at the right of the main hall open into the reception and dining hall. The gilt chairs with the national emblem painted on each one were handmade by craftsmen. The magnificent teak screen filling the bay window is carved with traditional Arabic emblems.

As well as the main reception building seen from the road, the palace contains a residential wing and a hall for state occasions. There is an interior courtyard where space has been devoted to a small but lush ornamental garden.

The Presidential Palace took two years to build. It was designed by a Malaysian architect and when the original design was presented to the government, modifications were made to suit the Maldivian style of architecture. Construction was by a Japanese company. Its furnishings represent the world's best in simple dignity.

The Palace is much larger than it seems when glimpsed from Orchid Magu and has been so strongly built it will last for centuries. It is a fitting symbol of the stature the Maldives has achieved in its transition from a forgotten Indian Ocean Sultanate to a dynamic and modern Islamic Republic.

Staying the Natural Way

The Impact of Tourism

"Tourists themselves have contributed most to making resort island operators environmentally aware and sensitive. They keep local and foreign developers on their toes."

The words were those of the man charged with responsibility for the environment, the former Minister of Planning, Human Resources and Environment, Ismail Shafeeu. He was commenting on the impact of tourism on the environment. While a law concerned with the preservation of the environment was passed by the Citizens' Majlis (parliament) in 1994, the negative effects of the tourist industry on the environment are seen as minimal.

"We have set up an Environmental Council which monitors the situation," said the Minister. "The tourist sector, however, has long been in the forefront of developing standards generally because of their high stake in ensuring a clean, safe environment."

The result is self-policing to preserve the idyllic environment that tourists enjoy, since the resorts, their guests and Maldivians all share the benefits. By regulation, every resort must have an incinerator, a metal can compactor and a bottle crusher as well as exercising care on where waste is dumped. Proper waste disposal is of vital importance as well as seeing the resort's reefs are protected.

The government has recognised the contribution the tourism industry is making in encouraging environmental awareness, with the introduction of awards presented on World Environment Day every year. The presentation of awards has helped make Maldivians, too, more conscious of the role they can play in helping to preserve the environment. In 1996, the Maldivian-owned Ihuru Tourist Resort was one of the recipients of an award from President Gayoom.

At Ihuru the owner estimates that the cost of running the resort in an ecologically responsible manner, adds about 30% to the room rate, compared with that charged in similar size resorts.

"Guests appreciate what we are doing. They often come up with ideas to help," said the owner, happy that the results of Ihuru's efforts, however small, are making the Maldives an even better place to be.

Even those who are not normally environment enthusiasts are choosing to stay at resorts where nature has its way. For the Maldives, it is clear that green is the colour of compatible tourism.

FACING PAGE
At the helm of his dhoni at dawn, the captain contemplates the day ahead.

GEGENÜBERLIEGENDE SEITE
Bei Sonnenaufgang ist der Kapitän am Steuer seines Dhonis in Gedanken an den vor ihm liegenden Tag versunken.

PAGINA A FRONTE
Al timone della sua dhoni all'alba, il comandante contempla il giorno davanti a sè.

The Rising Sea

"Although it is the subject of much scientific debate," said the Minister responsible for the environment, "there is a likelihood of a rise in the level of the sea caused by global warming. This is a consequence of industrialisation. We know the proportion of carbon gases discharged into the atmosphere by the USA, Japan, Germany... Visitors from those countries can look at the Maldives and make a judgement. They can decide on what they should do. The solution is in their hands."

Leave It Where It Is

This is the positive attitude to preserving the environment. Florets of coral that look so pretty underwater quickly become dull out of their natural setting. In the Maldives there is a list of prohibited marine products. The trade in and export of turtles and their products of any kind is banned, and so is the export of lobsters and lobster meat.

Even sport fishing practised by some resorts is now confined to the tag and release method.

The Human Resource

The Maldives is one of the few countries in the world low on what most countries have too much of: the human resource. The 1995 census recorded a population of 244,644. With the tourism industry expanding, there are more jobs than there are Maldivians who want them. Hence people from Sri Lanka, India, Bangladesh and Europe, as well as the Philippines, are hired on contract.

This is a result of the legacy of the island lifestyle before there was tourism. There were no social pressures or outside influences then on the inhabitants. There was enough to eat, and shelter: fishing brought in the income to raise a family. It still does. The World Bank described the Maldives as having always been in "a state of affluent subsistence."

While some of the educated youth can see the possibilities of career advancement in tourism, others who are equally capable prefer to run their own businesses.

Benefits have been funded, at least in part, by income generated through tourism. Another outcome of the first 25 years of the industry has been the broadening of options, enabling the school leaver to make a choice. Tourism provides many career opportunities, not just jobs for waiters and room boys.

Under the influence of visitors from the outside world, and through television too, the era of uncomplicated island existence has passed.

Fortunately, as young Maldivians enter the adult world, they are assured of a bright future, not the precarious existence (only the deluded romantic would call it lotus-eating) of a quarter of a century ago.

FACING PAGE
A signature image of the Maldives: the grace and simplicity of a dhoni *with curved prow in the clear waters of an island lagoon.*

GEGENÜBERLIEGENDE SEITE
Malediven wie aus dem Bilderbuch: die Eleganz und Schlichtheit eines Dhoni *mit gebogenem Bug in dem klaren Wasser einer Insellagune.*

PAGINA A FRONTE
Un'immagine - simbolo delle Maldive: la grazia e semplicità di una dhoni *dalla prua curva nelle acque limpide di una laguna insulare.*

ABOVE AND FACING PAGE
Complementing the sun, sand and sea, tropical fruits and flowers run riot in the islands. Above: Saplings for sale in a tree nursery, Male'. Facing page: (first and second rows, left to right) Hibiscus and breadfruit grow in resort islands and so do bougainvillaea and bananas. Bottom, left to right: Flowers in a resort and lush foliage in the Sultan's Park, Male'.

OBEN UND GEGENÜBERLIEGENDE SEITE
In Ergänzung zu Sonne, Sand und Wind finden sich tropische Früchte und Blumen in Hülle und Fülle auf den Inseln. Oben: Schößlinge werden zum Verkauf in einer Baumschule angeboten, Male; Gegenüberliegende Seite: (erste und zweite Reihe, von links nach rechts) Hibiskus und Brotfrucht wachsen auf Hotelinseln, ebenso Bougainvillea und Bananen. Unten, von links nach rechts: Blumen in einer Ferienanlage und üppige Vegetation im Park des Sultans, Male.

SOPRA E PAGINA A FRONTE
Non bastassero il sole, la spiaggia ed il mare, la frutta tropicale ed i fiori abbondano sulle isole. Sopra: piante in vendita in un vivaio, Malè. Pagina a fronte: (prima e seconda fila, da sinistra a destra) Ibisco e frutto del pane crescono sulle isole turistiche a fianco di bouganvillee e banane. Sotto, da sinistra a destra: Fiori in un villaggio, e il fogliame lussureggiante nel parco del Sultano a Malè.

One Million Trees

"In Male'," a resident said, "you either have a house or a garden. There is no space for both."

Yet Male' is not entirely a maze of concrete and coral buildings. Seen from the top floor of one of the new high-rise (well, eight storeys is high-rise in Male') it is surprisingly green.

There are trees wherever there is space for one. Some are tall and broad, blessing the courtyard in which it grows with shade. Some are nurtured carefully, others are left to fend for themselves, seeming to shrink when the weather is dry and hot, then greeting the rain with branches spread wide. These are trees that surprise by their resilience. Some are home to birds, like the huge flamboyants in the Sultan's Park where chattering parakeets gather in the afternoon.

No one knows how many trees there are in the Maldives, but by the end of this century there will be a million more. A nationwide programme to plant one million trees during a three-year period was launched in 1996 by the President.

In Male' a small nursery off Sosun Magu is where many of the trees for planting are being nurtured from cuttings. "Because of our type of soil," said one of the gardeners, "it takes a long time for a tree to grow."

Plants are offered for sale to the public to do their own tree planting. Small nurseries have been established in the atolls so that the programme spreads throughout the country.

There are regulations governing the felling of large, old trees and only coconut palm trees would be cut down to make space for houses or hotel rooms. Resort islands treasure as many trees as they can and are taking part in the programme by planting more palm, timber and fruit trees.

Nationally, the drive is under way to make the Maldives a million times greener.

The Park of the Sultans

A patch of greenery in the capital, Sultan's Park, is what remains of the garden of the Sultan's Palace. The palace buildings, except for what now houses the National Museum, were demolished when the Second Republic was created in 1968.

The park, only open on Friday afternoons, is a popular place for families and friends to stroll, and children to play, in the shade of giant flamboyant trees. Frangipani blossoms amidst bougainvillaea and oleander plants, and shaded paths wind their way through this botanical garden in miniature. There is a large cage of tropical birds, a fish pond and, in the park's centre, a fountain which forms a favoured backdrop for pictures taken on request by roving freelance photographers.

As the sun sets on Fridays, the park is packed with people relaxing among the flowers and trees. The gold-tipped minaret of the Islamic Centre can be glimpsed through the foliage, creating the impression of a haven of peace in a city that is at peace with itself.

Resort Gardens

As a contribution to improving the environment, many resorts have not only transformed what was an uninhabited coral island with infrastructure and buildings, but with gardens too. While some resorts opt for a rustic look with undergrowth and unswept paths, which may seem an easy way to avoid garden maintenance, others have landscaped mini botanical parks to complement the excellence of the accommodation.

Many islands are surprisingly lush, proving that with care flowers and trees will grow where, before an island became a resort, there was only sand and scrub. Gangehi has become a tropical jungle fantasy with boardwalks raised above the sand winding through clusters of palms, mangroves and exotic plants.

Kuramathi and Kunfunadhoo (now known as Sonevafushi resort) because of their size, have large tracts of natural tropical undergrowth and palm groves.

Avenues at Kuramathi have been enhanced with tropical blossoms adding the romantic touch to the environment. At Sonevafushi, no flowering plants are being introduced to disturb the ecology of the island although there are chickens and rabbits running wild.

Thick vegetation helps to hide the necessary intrusion into a Garden of Eden setting of a resort's rooms. This is done very successfully on the small island of Fesdu which somehow manages to contain, and conceal, 60 individual thatched cottages behind bougainvillaea bushes, palm trees and flourishing foliage. Many of the plants, as well as the soil in which they grow, are imported, along with the gardeners who care for them with so much dedication.

In fact, on every resort island, enhancing and encouraging the existing vegetation or creating special gardens is paramount.

Bananas and papayas are grown in some resorts, where there is space. In the Indian-run Biyadoo resort, horticulture has become a fine art. A hydroponic garden has been developed successfully with plants like tomatoes and cucumbers growing in troughs without soil. On its sister island of Villivaru each room boy is given the responsibility of tending the gardens in front of the room he services, leading to competition among the room boys for the best kept garden and adding beauty to an island of palm groves and shade trees.

The development of gardens on the resort islands results in displays of brilliant, if imported, flora. Because of this enhancement of the environment, fauna has benefited too. Bird life is scarce on many inhabited islands but in the nurtured vegetation of the resort islands, birds, mostly migrants, feel at home. Herons of various species can be seen wading or standing proudly and undisturbed by a resort's shore. Seagulls, terns and other seabirds abound. Lizards of ferocious demeanour, but actually harmless, scurry where gardens grow; geckoes thrive and keep back creepie-crawlies.

In the Maldives, tourism and the environment are compatible; it's nature's way.

Waste Not, Want Not

The matter of waste disposal is crucial to the successful development of holiday resorts on uninhabited islands. Whereas industrialised countries might channel their waste directly into the sea, the sea is the lifeblood of the Maldives and polluting it is to poison the whole country. No one worries about this more than the resort island operators.

Modern incinerators have been installed in many resorts to ensure efficient disposal of waste that cannot be recycled in some way. Leftover fruits, vegetables, leaves and other organic material is utilised to make compost. Cans are crushed, glass ground and used as a mix in concrete. The most ingenious methods have been devised to keep the islands beautiful and the sea free of garbage.

Sewerage is processed and miniature sewerage treatment plants are envisaged for developing resorts.

Where Fish Have a Chance

The fish have a chance in the Maldives: no nets are used to catch the skipjack and tuna which make up the bulk of the islands' exports. Fishing is done with a pole and line; the only bait used is live fish, which is scattered on the water to attract the tuna instead of dangling on hooks.

It is an inspired system of conservation, letting fish that would have been caught easily by net have a chance to survive, thereby breeding more fish. Since the fish caught every year by this painstaking routine is increasing, there seems to be method in the apparent madness. It protects marine resources as well as preventing the catching and extinction of other marine life, such as dolphins.

The importance of fish to the nation can easily be realised through a visit to the fish market in Male'. The day's catch is landed from *dhonis* in the afternoon and the sight of handcarts stacked with fish in rows being trundled through the town, is common. Fishing is done only during the day, and not on Fridays, with the fishermen returning to their island homes at night. The total catch each year is increasing and is now over 100,000 metric tons. About half the catch is exported.

The fishing industry, like tourism, has only developed since the 1970s. Up to then, all fishing craft (*masdhoni*) were sail powered and consequently were limited in where they could go by the whims of wind and tide. With mechanisation, *dhonis* were able to reach the fishing grounds faster and spend more time looking for fish. In the 12 hours spent at sea, more fish can be caught than in the days of sail.

Fishing vessels are from 10 to 15 metres long, locally made with timber, open decked and without a canopy. Each carries a crew of at least eight, only half of which will do the actual pole and line fishing, a skill that takes a lot of practice to master.

There are four main methods of fish processing: freezing, canning, smoking and drying, and salting. Fresh fish is, of course, sold locally but it is also collected and chilled to preserve its freshness, and airfreighted speedily to European and Far Eastern markets. This is done by MIFCO, the Maldives Industrial Fisheries Company and by private enterprise.

Canned tuna from the Maldives is in demand throughout the world although in your home supermarket the label of the product might not give its origins prominently and it will be marketed under a known domestic brand name. Since the fish is canned only when it is fresh, either in solid, chunked or flaked form, in soya bean oil, olive oil or brine, it preserves the real taste of the Maldives to enjoy at home.

The traditional method of smoking and drying yields a product known as Maldive Fish. This is popular in Asia, particularly in Sri Lanka, for adding flavour to spicy dishes. The cleaned, gutted and filleted fish is boiled in water containing salt and then smoked above a wood fire before being put in the sun to dry.

An independent Maldivian company markets dried tuna chips in colourful packs for visitors. The product has a wealth of vitamins and is 75.9% protein, 2.1% fat.

Gourmet delicacies like shark fins and sea cucumber are also part of the Maldives' exports of marine products to the world. The industry comes second in Gross Domestic Product (about 12%), to tourism (about 18%) and shares in the Maldives celebration as an industry that was reborn, although not started, in 1972.

The Underwater World

The Diving Dimension

The extra dimension that is the reason why more than 40% of tourists visit the Maldives is the underwater world. Now every resort has its own dive school and there are some schools in Male' too, with Maldivians among their pupils and instructors.

Diving, like tourism, has come a long way in 25 years. One of the first visitors to dive in the waters of the Maldives was Rainer F. Huth, who dived off Kurumba in 1974. He is still in the Maldives where he is regarded as the most experienced divemaster in the islands and is vastly respected for his knowledge of the underwater world. He is the chairman of the Scuba Diving Association of the Maldives, to which most resort schools are affiliated.

Rainer Huth has recalled that life for visitors was very informal in the early 1970s, and diving was the same. He returned in 1975 and spent a year, in two stages, travelling through all the atolls from north to south, getting to know the waters. He opened his first diving school at Kuramathi in 1977.

"Diving became really popular," he said, "when charter flights began arriving in the Maldives, making the islands easily accessible to people who wanted to dive."

He has noticed that divers have become very concerned about the marine environment and take good care of it. On several dives off Kuramathi to clean up the reefs as part of World Environment Day observance in 1996, he and other divers found only two iron pipes, one plastic bottle and 10 metres of fishing line. It proves divers care.

One of his favourite dives which thrills visitors is only 10 minutes away from Kuramathi. It is an early morning dive to swim with hammerhead sharks. He has been observing them for 10 years and delights in introducing visitors to share the experience.

The Maldives has won praise from divers and the world's tourism industry for its environment friendly tourism.

FACING PAGE
Within a week, even beginners can learn to scuba dive and follow fish underwater.

GEGENÜBERLIEGENDE SEITE
Sogar Anfänger können innerhalb einer Woche das Tauchen erlernen und die Unterwasserwelt erkunden.

PAGINA A FRONTE
Entro una settimana anche i principianti sono in grado di imparare la pesca subacquea e di seguire i pesci sott'acqua.

"Tourism, since its inception," Shaahina, a local diving instructor has written, "has focused around the fragile marine environment. More than 60% of visitors go diving. The Ministry of Tourism with the resort operators have in many ways played a very important role in preserving eco-friendly tourism that is expanding rapidly.

"The underwater landscape is the most varied, rich and definitely the most colourful feature of these beautiful islands. Whether it is just swimming with a goggle, snorkelling or diving, exploring the magnificent underwater world is what attracts the thousands who visit the Maldives every year. Countless are the numbers of young and old who have forgotten their fear and taken up diving here, becoming fascinated with the attractive fish and coral life, and the simplicity of it all.

"Diving is the most thrilling experience for visitors. A first dive is enough to leave a lasting memory. The coral that forms reefs intricately entwines with other organisms to create the base reef with enough colour to take your breath away.

"Fish life, from tiny cleaner shrimps to the huge whale shark, could all be sighted on one dive if you are lucky. Eels, sharks, sting rays, manta rays, napoleon wrasse and whale sharks are the biggest attractions and even the little bristle worms on the corals have their fascination.

"Dive sites of Maldives such as Shark Point, Manta Point, Hammerhead Point, Lion's Head and Banana Reef, are well known around the world among the diving community. All are protected.

"For the visitor to the Maldives, diving becomes a must, even if it was not the original intention for coming here. Each resort offers diving courses to clients through well equipped dive schools. Prices vary from resort to resort. A novice could obtain a PADI or similar openwater licence in about a week.

"Expansion in the marine based economy of the islands was in danger of affecting reef and fish life. With large amounts of sharks and groupers being fished for export, divers reported that fish were disappearing from popular dive locations.

"To save the marine resources that had become the bedrock of tourism, in 1995 the government declared 15 prominent dive sites as areas protected from economic exploitation, including fishing and coral mining."

This move ensures not only an undisturbed environment for marine life, but also a chance for those who venture underwater to observe it.

Maldive Cuisine: Tasty Dishes with Fish

Short Eats

"Whatever we eat in the Maldives is fish," said our guide to the short eats, or little snacks (*hedhikaa*), neatly set out on small plates in the tea shop on the Male' waterfront.

We had dropped in for a cup of tea, a pleasant custom in Male' whenever friends meet. With the cups of tea go snacks of some kind, chosen from a range laid out on the table for customers to choose what they want.

There were a dozen different kinds in front of us, most grouped in fours on plates since charging is done on the basis of how many items are eaten from each four. Those around the table help themselves; the waiter counts what has been consumed and, when asked for it, brings the bill written on a square of paper.

That fish should be the mainstay of Maldivian cuisine is no surprise since it is one of the few food items that is found locally. Locally-grown green vegetables are in short supply and this is reflected in every meal on the islands. However, with imported items freely available now, eggs and vegetables as well as beef and chicken are often seen on tea shop tables in Male'.

Coconut, being plentiful, is a major ingredient in snacks, either grated and squeezed to provide the liquid for binding flour or cooking, or for flavouring curries. The grated flesh is used in savoury and sweet delights.

The snacks in Male' tea shops are a sample of the broader range of Maldivian cuisine and proof of the ingenuity of Maldivian cooks in dressing up fish so that it remains attractive, even to people who have it for breakfast, lunch and dinner.

A traditional favourite with a spicy kick to it is called *kulhi boakibaa. Kulhi* means hot and *boakibaa* refers to the baked cake, usually served as squares cut from a large, firm pudding-like slab. Onions, chilli, ginger and coconut—the ingredients that are the staple of most Maldivian recipes—are mixed with the seasoned rice and

FACING PAGE
A dhoni *unloads its day's catch at the quay opposite the fish market in Male'.*

smoked fish (*valhoamas*) to produce this satisfying fish cake.

Another kind of *boakibaa* is made from rice that has been soaked overnight and seasoned liberally with *rihaakuru*, the rich concentrated tuna fish paste that looks like Marmite.

There is a sweet version, called *foni boakibaa* made from flour, water and sugar. Another version, baked separately in individual moulds, with egg and raisins added, is known as *Misuru* (Egypt) *boakibaa*. It has the almond-like nuts, *kanamadhu*, placed on top.

There are various kinds of fish snacks, all made with a mix of shredded fish plus seasoning as their filling, presented in different shapes. Round like a fat coin is *kavaabu*. The ball-shaped snacks are *gulha* which have a stuffing of *valhomas* with coconut, ginger, onions, chilli and lime juice encased in a rice-flour dough which is hard and crusty through shallow frying. This is called *handulu gulha*. There are several varieties of *gulha*, including those with a softer coating made of wheat flour.

Snacks that look like Chinese spring rolls are based on the same fish and spices mix, with the addition of potatoes. The covering is like a batter and the rolls, actually called *keemiya*, are deep fried. *Masfathafolhi* is also a fish (*mas*) snack with breadfruit and vegetable, packeted in baked pastry.

Mas roshi is baked, circular in shape, like a flattened scone. It has a stuffing of fish mixture with *kulhlhafilaafaiy*, a green leaf, added to give it zest.

Rihafolhi is tasty since it consists of a dry curry of fish and spices rolled up in a soft, yellow crêpe made of eggs and flour. The triangular shaped fried snacks (like samousa) are plump and stuffed with a filling of fish and spices. They are known as *bajiya*. Another fried, envelope-shaped short eat is one of the few that does not have fish. Instead, chopped boiled egg and cabbage with black pepper are combined into a filling to make a snack called *biskeemiya*.

Sweet items to be found on tea shop tables in Male' are very colourful. The bright pink whorl is *zileybee*. It is basically a batter of flour and sugar piped through a nozzle into hot oil in a catherine-wheel design and fried. The bright yellow batter confection moulded in the shape of a miniature car's chassis is popular in India and known locally as *kaajaa*.

Longer Eats

Cooking in a village island is usually done over a wood fire in the grate of an outhouse, with chimney. This is traditionally located away from the main residence because of the risk from fire when houses were made of thatch, and to reduce the inconvenience from smoke. Even where gas stoves have replaced the wood fire, and cement blocks have ousted thatch, the kitchen is usually in a separate building.

High above the traditional wood fire grate is a grill on which is placed fish so that it gets smoked at the same time that the fire is being used for cooking. Smoked fish, *valhoamas*, is a breakfast dish. When it is shredded and combined with coconut, onion, chilli, lime juice and with some kind of green leaf, it is called *Mas huni*. This is eaten dry with *roshi*. *Roshi* is a flat, pancake-style bread made of flour, water, oil and salt, kneaded into a dough. The dough is rolled out into thin rounds and prepared

over a hot griddle.

Roshi is an alternative to the ubiquitous rice for a main meal. Four *roshi*, or more, are torn up, almost ritually, by the diner and placed on a plate. Curry is then poured over the scraps of *roshi*, mixed and the meal is eaten with the fingers. A rice substitute in the south, is *taro*, a yam, which, fried crisply, can also be eaten as a snack. Breadfruit, too, is a staple on the islands where it is grown and can be eaten as a vegetable, fried in chips, or as the constituent of a sweet dish called *bodibai*.

Rice is served at every main meal. It is usually plain, boiled white rice served with *rihaakuru* or with curry, if available. *Rihaakuru* is prepared by boiling down tuna fish stock until it concentrates into a paste.

The favourite relish is not curry, though, but a clear, bland liquid which could be mistaken for soup. This is *garudhiya* and has chunks of tuna fish floating in it. This liquid is poured over rice which has been cooked with coconut milk, and mixed into it with the fingers. Lime and raw chilli is added at the table to get the piquancy required. Locally made pickle, *asaara*, is also eaten with this dish.

Eating Out

When tourism was beginning in the 1970s, tourists used to bring sandwiches and tinned food with them because they were worried they would find nothing to eat. The Maldivian diet of fish and rice, or rice and fish, soon became boring for palates used to greater variety. Cooks were hired from overseas and supplies brought in especially for tourist consumption.

Over the years, Maldivians have themselves been trained in the cuisines tourists prefer, and on most islands the majority of the kitchen staff is Maldivian. This gives a chance for visitors to try good Maldivian food at their resorts (usually on special Maldivian theme nights) instead of having to go to Male' to visit the tea shops.

Most resort islands offer a rate for full board (room and all meals) or half board (room, breakfast and dinner). A set menu usually consists of a starter, soup and a main course, together with dessert and tea or coffee. Some meals are presented as buffets. Even the smallest resort will have a separate area for snacks as extras for the peckish. The plushest resorts boast restaurants with an à la carte menu.

The gourmet is not neglected. There are specialist restaurants on some resorts featuring Thai, Chinese, Indian, Japanese and Continental fine dining. Even in Male' where the patrons are more likely to be Maldivians than tourists, there are restaurants with Italian, Indian and Thai specialities as well as good steaks in the city's hotel restaurants.

Seafood addicts won't be disappointed although the prawns and crabs are imported. Squids and octopuses do come from local waters, and sometimes locally-caught lobsters are available at resorts.

The chefs in every resort are keen to cater to any culinary requests, challenging the Male' tea shops with food that is a delight to the eye as well as a treat to eat. You can safely leave the sandwiches at home.

The Magic of Male'

A Capital in Transition

Male' casts its spell the moment you glimpse it from the sea. The golden dome of the Islamic Centre glistens in the sunlight, new buildings thrust skywards in solitary splendour beside one-storey blocks of offices and shops. The capital seems to be rising from the ocean as your vessel draws near. You can only arrive, and leave, by boat so Male' with its bustling waterfront exerts its strange fascination over everyone.

In the hot, remorseless sun beating down on people walking its streets, or when a rain shower catches the unwary, the city's magic may seem a far-fetched fantasy. Male' is not a pretty city, but it is a clean one. People may move slowly in its streets, but in its airconditioned offices there is a quiet dynamism. The stranger senses Male' is a capital in transition; there is always something new being built. Visitors become attached to Male'; they feel they are making a personal discovery of a place with a future, a city on the verge of great potential.

Part of the capital's charm can be derived from walking its streets and being inspired by the thought that this is how most cities began, in a small, slow way. You can see Male' growing: the coral stone cottage on the corner today will be transformed into a three-storey, airconditioned, glass-fronted office building with a penthouse apartment by tomorrow. Change is inevitable; in Male' it is incredible.

Within living memory, the streets of the capital were sand and its houses *cadjan* (palm-thatched) shacks. The main complex was the Sultan's, with a granite block fort and cannons to protect it. The fort's walls fell in the 1960s, attacked by the demolition crews' hammers, not by an invader's blows. The surrender of Male' to the future was swift.

Within a decade, the 1970s, a self-contained village was transformed into a city capital. The town the first tourists saw 25 years ago would be only vaguely familiar to them today.

Male' has always been the main island of the Maldives although why it is called Male' (written with an apostrophe, not an acute accent although it is pronounced Mar-lay) is not clear. Some say it is a contraction of Malei, referring to the dynasty which ruled the archipelago 800 years ago. Others see it as a combination of words of different meanings.

FACING PAGE
Male' has expanded to twice its natural size to accommodate those who want to live in the capital.

GEGENÜBERLIEGENDE SEITE
Males ursprüngliche Größe hat sich inzwischen verdoppelt, um den Andrang all derer, die es in die Hauptstadt zieht, zu bewältigen.

PAGINA A FRONTE
Malè si è ingrandita del doppio rispetto alla sua estensione originaria, per accontentare quelli che vogliono vivere nella capitale.

There are not many who cling to the past in Male'; only a few private residences of antique style remain. Those that do are hidden behind high walls, safe, probably only temporarily, from the emerging future. There are no classic cars in the streets lingering from the 1960s, although they did exist in Male' then. Instead, cars are the latest models imported from Japan. Even the junk offered for sale in the informal "flea market" under trees by the vegetable market, is modern. There are electric typewriters and video cassettes, no 1920s' Remingtons or gramaphone records.

You get the feeling that Male' having lived in the past for so long, is determined to forget it now and get on with the future. And why not? There are streetside pay-card telephones from where you can call directly to anywhere in the world. Yet only a few years ago, the only communication link was by radio telephone.

Male' is fascinating to visitors from abroad because of the infrastructure they know. They see familiar technology on a two square kilometre flat coral island in the Indian Ocean and are amazed. Male' proves that progress and prosperity and efficiency are not solely the prerogative of developed countries in Europe. It is part of the incredible magic of Male' that this small over-populated island can teach the world about coexistence and courtesy, qualities rare in the competitive, stress-filled societies tourists come from.

Male' is probably the safest, least stressful capital in the modern world. Anyone can walk the streets day or night without harassment or hassle. You move at a leisurely pace whether walking or cocooned in an airconditioned taxi. It takes only 20 minutes to walk from one side of the island to another; a stroll around the island by the sea wall takes an hour.

Male' shops remain open until late at night, and the evening streets are full of promenaders. While government offices close at 2.30 pm, they open at 7.30 am so work starts early. Private offices sometimes close in the afternoon and re-open again in the evening, getting two days' work from one. The working week is Sunday to Thursday. There are prayer breaks in the afternoon and evening.

Many resort islands organise shopping trips to Male' which gives visitors a chance to see the capital. The boats bringing them are met at the waterfront by personable young men as guides who are fluent in many languages and explain a little of Male's history. Just five minutes' walk inland from the waterfront is the Hukuru Miskiiy, also known as Friday mosque. It was constructed of coral stone in 1656 on the site of the country's first mosque built in 1153.

The sloping roof and the intricate carvings on the coral blocks of the building's exterior are all that most visitors see since special permission is required to enter the mosque. Inside it radiates an atmosphere of deep reverence. It has heavy wooden doors that slide open to inner sanctums glimpsed through ancient lattice work; the ceiling is elaborately carved from wood, complementing the wood and stone pillars of its interior. The floor is carpeted and the mosque is used for contemplation and prayer since its replacement by the Islamic Centre in 1984 as Male's main place of worship.

Although much larger mosques (some even with airconditioning) have been built over the years, the Hukuru Miskiiy has retained its importance because of its links with the past. As one of the few ancient buildings remaining in Male', it symbolises

MALE'

INDIAN OCEAN

Customs

Fishing Dhonis & Inter-Atoll Vessels

Fishmarket

Inner Harbour

Presidential Jetty

STO Shopping Complex

Jumhooree Maidan

Boduthakurufaanu Magu (Marine Drive)

Dhonis For Hire

Dhonis

Presidential Palace

Tourist Shopping Area

Islamic Centre

Friday Mosque

Ministry of Tourism

Boat Yard

Munnarru

Meduzaraiy Magu

Dhiraagu Telecom Centre

Mulee-aage

Medhu Ziyaaraiy

Museum & Sultan's Park

Orchid Magu

Fareedi Magu

Chandhani Magu

Institute of Hotel & Catering Services

Sosun Magu

Post Shop

Clock Tower

Bihroaz Kamana Miskiiy

Majeedi Magu

Majeedi Magu

National Stadium

Sosun Magu

Tomb of Ali Rasgefaanu

Indira Gandhi Memorial Hospital

Mast

Mast

Surfing

Tetrapod Monument

Southern Harbour

Swimming Area

INDIAN OCEAN

N

the continuity of the Maldivian culture and faith. The legion of headstones around it and the sepulchres sheltering the remains of noble personages of the past bear witness to this link.

The stout, round tower of classic proportions outside the mosque compound is the minaret, built in 1675 and resembling minarets of the time in Mecca. The call to prayer used to be made from the top of this tower by the *mudhim* who climbed it five times a day. In 1964 loudspeakers were installed and the *mudhim* broadcast his call while standing inside the mosque.

Across the road is the blue and white building that is the shrine called Medhu Ziyaaraiy. The Moroccan traveller Abul Barakaath Yoosuf Al Barbary, who is credited with converting the country to Islam, is commemorated by this memorial and it is regarded as a sacred site in this very historical area of Male'.

Adjacent to it is Mulee-aagee, the official residence of the President until 1994. It was built in 1906 by the reigning sultan, replacing a house on the same site dating back to the mid-17th century. Its exterior with protruding wings and a central verandah is reminiscent of the architectural style of the same period in neighbouring Sri Lanka.

A short walk westwards takes you to the Sultan's Park and the gold-tipped minaret of the Islamic Centre. In a way the museum which is in Sultan's Park reflects the mood of the city.

It is small and homely with priceless treasures on display without any security, apart from an old guardian who shows visitors around. Some objects have explanations in English, others don't. There is a mixture of exhibits from ancient stone carvings to bullet-holed motorbikes. It is, like Male', a trove of the unexpected, giving a wealth of insight into a country whose past a visitor might otherwise overlook.

The Edwardian-style building with narrow wooden staircases climbing through its three floors, is all that remains of the Sultan's Palace. A model layout shows how the entire complex, complete with ramparts and cannons, used to look. The lifestyle of the sultans can be imagined from the trappings of office (ceremonial umbrellas, turbans, thrones and tunics) remaining as exhibits. There is a palanquin, a bed from a tomb, a gunpowder chest; all manner of extraordinary artefacts that hint at a past of both grace and drama.

Across the road is the Islamic Centre whose golden-hued dome dominates the skyline and is an eye-catching reminder of the reality of the island's faith. Built in 1984, the three-storey centre houses an Islamic Library, a conference hall, classrooms and the Grand Mosque, named after Sultan Muhammad Thakurufaanu.

The architecture is simple but elegant, its uncluttered lines emphasised by the expanse of broad steps leading up to interior galleries overlooking the vast, carpeted prayer hall. The mosque is the largest in the Maldives, and can accommodate 5,000 people, many gathering outside on the terraces, in prayer. Around its main prayer hall are woodcarvings and Arabic calligraphy, some designed by President Gayoom, etched by Maldivian craftsmen as a testimony of dignity and beauty to their faith.

The road from the Islamic Centre to the waterfront crosses the open space now known as Jumhooree Maidan (Republic Square), a pleasant park surrounded by shade trees and stone benches where people wait for friends or the *dhonis* that ply

between Male' and the resorts. Opposite is the Presidential Jetty with its elaborately carved wooden canopy commanding access to the waterfront boulevard.

A feature of modern Male' is its roads which are paved like pedestrian-only precincts, with solid bricks fitted into the sand like a jigsaw in a herringbone pattern. There are about 50,000 bicycles registered in the Maldives (most of them in Male') and they dodge with ease between the capital's necessarily slow-moving cars. There are about 2,000 motor vehicles (not including 4,500 motorcycles) registered in the whole of the Maldives, of which the majority are in Male'.

A walk along Orchid Magu, which diverts southwesterly from the beginning of Chandhani Magu, leads to Male's most impressive building, the Presidential Palace, called Theemuge. Also in Orchid Magu is the State Trading Organisation (STO) Plaza, a multi-storied centre with a supermarket on its ground floor.

At the other side of the block are several lanes of small grocery-cum-hardware stores where residents from the fishing village islands like to stock up during their visits to Male'. The lanes lead to the markets on the waterfront.

A haven of shade in the city is the local market whose green sidings filter the glare of the sun and create an atmosphere of tranquillity. There is neither shouting by vendors, nor the bustle of buying, only the unhurried rhythm of occasional commerce as shoppers choose from the bunches of bananas hanging by string from the roof, or select a pumpkin or two. The range of vegetables is actually small, very little locally grown produce reaching the Male' market. But treats are plentiful with packets of sweetmeats, nuts and other goodies.

In the open-air square outside the market, beside the road where inter-island vessels nudge the waterfront wall, trading is brisker. Firewood, coconuts and tin water dippers are on offer together with shark jaw bones and special bargains of shirts or shoe polish, or whatever items the vendors have garnered for sale. The fish market, washed clean at night, is lusty with trading as the sun sets and *dhonis* tie up at the quay to unload their day's catch. As fast as fish is brought in, it is gutted and sold, taken away in handcarts or simply hung from a bicycle's handlebars as the purchaser pedals home.

Westwards along the waterfront, past solid, squat godowns turned into stores and offices, is the customs wharf where cargo from ships anchored in the roadstead is unloaded. Walk on, and on, under the spell of discovering a city you can encircle in an hour, and you can take the waterfront road right around the island.

Past the Maldives Centre for Social Education is the Indira Gandhi Memorial Hospital, with 200 beds, newly built in a stunning shape with a hipped roof curving up in the shape of a *dhoni*'s sails. It looks impressive when viewed from the sea and offers upgraded health care for the general public. Private health care is also available at the other side of the island in Sosun Magu.

On the southern corner of Male' is another harbour, a new addition providing space for the hundreds of vessels that visit the capital to stay for a few nights. Safari cruise vessels pause there between voyages, alongside the broad-beamed wooden inter-atoll passenger and cargo boats, and smaller trading *dhonis*.

This is Male's own version of a fashionable Mediterranean marina but it harbours the working vessels of the islands, not the floating palaces of jet-setters. It remains undiscovered by the world's yachting fraternity.

At the eastern end is Dharubaaruge (which means coronation hall). This was built for the Fifth summit, held in 1990, of the South Asian Association for Regional Cooperation (SAARC). This organisation links the Maldives with Bangladesh, Bhutan, India, Nepal, Pakistan and Sri Lanka. It is seen as an important forum for the country's advancement.

Children splash in the swimming pool formed by the calming of the sea where breakwaters run parallel to the shore. "Every child swims" is the slogan inspiring them as they leap with spirit off the quay. Daring boys bodysurf at the eastern corner. There, an open space forms a recreation area. A concrete four-limbed tetrapod weighing three tons is set as a monument commemorating the building with tetrapods to protect the foreshore.

Inland off Majeedhee Magu is the National Stadium, venue for the many football tournaments played enthusiastically between city, and sometimes visiting, teams. Football is almost an obsession with Male's youth; it knows no seasons.

Male', being small and surrounded by sea, is appropriately shipshape; everything has its place in a neat and trim order. It is compact and secure, a serene, family-size city; one that a stranger will feel safe and at home in very easily. That's the magic of Male' in this modern world.

Defined by the Sea

Beyond Male', every inhabited island is a village defined by the sea. The sea governs not just its boundaries but also its way of life. The sea is the source of food and of shelter; it is the highway to neighbouring villages.

The woman's role in the village extends beyond housekeeping to keeping the family together. With a husband gone fishing all day, or away for months if he is working on an island resort, she has responsibility for introducing the children to their faith and seeing they are properly clothed and educated. She is helped in this by the older women, who each share in doing the family chores.

Supplies are few since village shops stock only the basics. Each meal is a fresh task, with coconuts having to be scraped and spices pounded; wood collected and the fire lit; fish cleaned, dough kneaded and pots scoured.

With their men absent, the women engage quietly in their own occupations. Coral flotsam may have to be sorted and heaped for use in construction, or coconut husks beaten into the coir used for mattress stuffing or plaited into ropes. Fish is dried, mats are woven, containers made from reeds, clothes handstitched into modest garments.

Men who are fishing leave the island early in the morning, after prayers, and return only at nightfall. Prayers will not be forgotten, even at sea, and at noon the devout will move to the bow and pray to Mecca.

Marriage is simple and there is no dowry system. After marriage, a woman can retain her maiden name. Death is dealt with swiftly, burial being within 24 hours. Birthdays are not rated as special occasions in a village; more important is the circumcision ceremony. This normally takes place during the long school holidays beginning in December and is disguised as a jolly time with games and music to distract the boys in a group from the trauma. Circumcision is usually performed when a boy reaches six or seven years and is considered the most important moment in a boy's life.

There are primary schools on every inhabited island and the realisation of the benefits to be gained from education is strong. The literacy rate is high, at about 98%.

FACING PAGE
An islander keeps his eye on the world from his palm-thatched cottage.

GEGENÜBERLIEGENDE SEITE
Ein Insulaner betrachtet die Welt von seiner palmengedeckten Hütte aus.

PAGINA A FRONTE
Un isolano tiene d'occhio il mondo dalla sua abitazione dal tetto di palma.

The beach and the sea are the playgrounds for most children. Where there is space, there will be a playing field used for football. Most islands have some form of social club whose members contribute to the welfare and development of their village.

Each island has a chief, usually a distinguished island citizen, appointed by the government. According to the island's size, he will be assisted by a number of full-time officials. In a small community, a chief (or *katheeb*) knows all that is happening on his island. The community is self-policing, help being sought from the National Security Service (NSS) only when necessary. A magistrate deals with criminal and legal matters.

Each of the administrative atolls is governed by an atoll chief. He is an official of importance appointed, in the same manner as ministers and ambassadors, by the President. He has a role similar to that of a provincial governor.

No island is simply coconut palms, coral stone cottages and the sybaritic lifestyle of castaway dreams. There are codes of conduct, both formal and informal, which serve to maintain good neighbourly behaviour in the confines of an island. Villagers are by nature conservative.

Neither are the islands primitive, since government programmes bring the benefits of development to every one. Larger islands have houses set out in blocks like an urbanisation scheme. Islands are split by well-maintained streets, albeit of sand. There are motor vehicles on some islands, motorbikes on a few and pedal cycles on others. Every island will have a telephone by the end of the century .

Village relaxation is simply sitting down, but in style. Each village has a variety of seating arrangements. The most common is the *joali*. This is a standing frame webbed with coir rigging to form individual bucket-type seats. They are usually

revenusd.

found outside the village houses for villagers to relax and enjoy the breeze.

Communal relaxing is done on a *holhu-ashi*. With a shelter of a tree's branches, this is a raised platform of logs usually located on the beach or close to it in a central part of the village. Village men gather to relax together, playing chess or cards, or just to sleep. Since everybody patronises the *holhu-ashi* sometimes, important notices for the villagers' attention are often tacked onto the sheltering tree's trunk.

For tourists it is possible to visit inhabited islands close to the resorts. This is usually on designated days by organised trips, which enables the islanders to adapt to visitors disrupting their daily routine. What this means is that when they know tourists are coming, islanders set up stalls in the main street, offering modest souvenirs. There are even proper souvenir shops if the island is frequently visited.

Boduberu Beat

A change comes over the community when the *boduberu* beat throbs through the cool evening air. Villagers flock to watch the show, never failing to be stirred by the irresistible drumming, even if the lyrics are as much a mystery to them as they are to foreigners. The songs are a mixture of local, neighbouring and African words, a derivation of chants and incantations introduced centuries ago by seafarers and settlers from Africa.

While *boduberu* may seem spontaneous—and visitors seeing a performance in resorts cannot resist joining in—it follows a practised pattern. A *boduberu* group usually consists of 15 people, including three drummers and a lead singer. Dancing to the drum beat and voice is by members of the group who revel in expressing themselves with grotesque and satirical postures. The climax builds gradually to a frenzy of frantic movements which inevitably leads participants to a trance, not always faked.

Boduberu has been described as "vibrating the island". As a means of letting off steam, and providing entertainment for fellow villagers, it is as much a sport as a dance, whatever its origins. Other folk dances typical of village life are now more usually seen in government sponsored cultural festivals.

Dressing for the Occasion

The women leave the dancing to the men although they will watch with interest. While the men wear sarongs and (a recent addition) T-shirts both to dance and as their daily work clothes, women are more circumspect. Older women prefer a wraparound cloth as a skirt that is tucked in at the waist and worn, like a petticoat, under a long-sleeved dress of a bold colour that reaches just below the knees. For a more formal occasion, the front and back of the neckline of this outfit is usually embroidered with fine lines of golden thread.

The traditional hairstyle matching this outfit is with a bun on the right side of the head. More fashionable than traditional is the modest and attractive dress known as *faaskuri hedhun* or *dhigu hedhun*. This is a long-sleeved dress that reaches the ankles, rather like a glamorous ball gown. A scarf, pinned to the hair and usually matching the hair's length goes with this outfit, like a trailing veil.

Take Away Maldives

The Souvenir Search

The most popular souvenir from the Maldives seems to be a T-shirt. At least it has the virtue of being designed and printed in the Maldives, even if the garment itself was produced elsewhere.

There was no souvenir industry before tourism, although handicrafts for local use were produced on a small scale. The rise of the T-shirt industry was in response to demands by visitors.

Unable to afford proper T-shirt printing equipment, young Maldivian artists went into business for themselves using island technology: substitute materials. Stencils were made out of found waste, like X-ray film. Sponges and even rags were used to dab on ordinary paint through the cut stencils.

Each T-shirt was an individual expression by the artist and those first T-shirts were a unique island art form. Some young people did so well with their T-shirt shops in Male' and in the resorts, that they went on to open their own souvenir shops. Meanwhile, with modern technology, T-shirt printing has become a big business.

A search for souvenirs in the tourist-oriented shops in Male' reveals a wealth of mementos from Asia to take away. You will find brightly coloured wooden fish mobiles from Indonesia, exotic wooden masks and gift packed tea from Sri Lanka and onyx work from India. The range on offer is eclectic, representing the best from the region. There are traditional handicrafts too, such as lacquer work, delicate basketware, silver and gold wire jewellery, woven mats, but these, being hand-made, are in short supply.

Highly-prized would be one of the beautifully woven *thundu kuna* (mats) made from reeds, a craft peculiar to islands in Huvadhu Atoll. The mats are woven freestyle contained by a rope frame pegged out to embrace the warp, or on a wooden loom. Coloured reeds are used as the weft. The reeds are grown on the islands.

Smaller versions of the mats are made by a weaver from Gadhdhoo who demonstrates her skill at the resort of Bandos. She deftly scrapes the reeds before threading them into the warp and ramming home the weft with a swing of the wooden loom.

FACING PAGE

Mats of woven screwpine, like these made in Kihaadhoo, adorn the walls, floors and ceilings of many island resorts.

GEGENÜBERLIEGENDE SEITE

Matten aus geflochtener Schraubenpalme wie diese, hergestellt in Kihaadhoo, schmücken die Wände, Fußböden und Decken vieler Ferienanlagen auf den Inseln.

PAGINA A FRONTE

Stuoie di pandan, come queste fatte a Kihaadhoo, adornano le pareti, i pavimenti ed i soffitti delle abitazioni in molti villaggi turistici.

BELOW
Souvenir shops in Chandhani Magu, Male'.

FACING PAGE
Top and bottom left: Goldsmiths at work in Male' producing beautiful souvenirs. Bottom right: A young man works patiently on the intricate designs of lacquerware from Thulaadhoo.

UNTEN
Andenkenladen in Chandhani Magu, Male.

GEGENÜBERLIEGENDE SEITE
Oben und unten links: Goldschmiede bei der Arbeit in Male stellen wunderschöne Andenken her. Unten rechts: Ein junger Mann arbeitet geduldig an dem aufwendigen Design einer Thulaadhoo-Lackarbeit.

SOTTO
Un negozio di souvenir a Chandhani Magu, Malè.

PAGINA A FRONTE
Sopra e sotto a sinistra: Orafi al lavoro a Malè nella produzione di souvenirs. Sotto a destra: Un giovane lavora pazientemente all'intricato disegno delle lacche di Thulaadhoo.

The most attractive locally-made souvenir is lacquerware. This is an ancient craft with renowned work coming from Thulaadhoo in Baa Atoll. There, a few craftsmen of advanced years keep alive a craft taught to them by their grandfathers. Some young men have shown interest too but little of their work reaches the souvenir shops. At the resort island of Bandos, a craftsman works full time producing wooden vases, containers and goblets that, with their lacquer sheen, look like fragile glass.

The technique is for a block of wood to be handcarved into the object to be lacquered. The lathe is manpowered, by an assistant who pulls a rope around a spindle backwards and forwards in a steady rhythm to turn the wheel on which is fastened the block of wood. The woodcarver works quickly with ancient tools, his dexterity transforming the wood into a desired, and exciting, object. After sandpapering it smooth, he burnishes in the coloured lacquer while the wheel is turned at speed.

Designs in black and gold resembling Chinese filigree motifs take longer to produce. Easier are wooden pill and trinket boxes in unusual colours or with red and yellow rings around them. Chess pieces are also made in laquerware but are almost impossible to find to buy since it takes so long to make a complete set. The pieces have to be handshaped on a hand-operated lathe with the same technique carpenters use to make divots, the pegs in a *dhoni* around which ropes are tied. The divot shape of the chess pieces, with only size to distinguish which one is which, makes chess, Maldivian style, additionally challenging.

BELOW

No trains in the Maldives but the country's modern thematic stamps, as seen on this First Day Cover, appeal to collectors worldwide. Below right: The oldest stamp from the Maldives, an overprint of a Ceylon stamp issued in 1906. The palm tree stamp dates from 1950.

UNTEN

Zwar gibt es auf den Malediven keine Züge, doch die Briefmarken zeigen stattdessen moderne Thematik, wie z.B. auf dieser Erstausgabe, und wecken damit das Interesse von Briefmarkensammlern in aller Welt. Unten rechts: Die älteste Briefmarke der Malediven, ein Aufdruck auf einer ceylonesischen Briefmarke, die 1906 herausgegeben wurde. Die Palmenbriefmarke stammt aus dem Jahre 1950.

SOTTO

Non ci sono treni alle Maldive ma i recenti francobolli a tema, come si vede in questa commemorazione del Primo Giorno, attraggono i collezionisti di tutto il mondo. Sotto a destra: Il più vecchio francobollo delle Maldive, una riproduzione di un francobollo di Ceylon emesso nel 1906. Il francobollo con la palma risale al 1950.

A Stamp in Time

The simplest souvenirs of the Maldives are postage stamps. Although they are actually printed in the UK many are designed in the Maldives, by Maldivians, to special Maldivian themes.

At the Post Shop in Male' there is a special philatelic section where first-day covers and souvenir issues of stamps can be purchased. Since some stamps are designed for thematic collectors, not all feature scenes typical of the Maldives. For instance, the Trains of Asia series issued in 1994 is fascinating both for train fans and also for Maldivians, most of whom have never been on a train.

The first postage stamp used in the Maldives was dated 1906 when the postal service was introduced. It records the British connection through Ceylon since the stamps were actually those in use in Ceylon at the time with "Ceylon" heavily overprinted in black ink with "Maldives". A portrait of Edward VII in profile appears on them and they are much prized by collectors.

In 1909 a set of 12 different coloured and valued stamps, all featuring the same scene of the minaret of the Hukuru Miskiiy, were issued. These were the first stamps dedicated to the Maldives and were in circulation for 24 years. The replacement issue showing a palm tree and sailing boat remained in use for 17 years.

Various pictorial issues followed, including a fortuitous occasion to commemorate in the Maldives as early as 1967: International Tourism Year. So there was a stamp issued in the Maldives to celebrate world tourism five years before world tourism discovered the Maldives. Another issue to commemorate tourism was released in 1984. Other postal souvenirs, such as Maldives thematic stamps set in plastic as a key fob, postal service caps and, yes, stamp T-shirts, are also available.

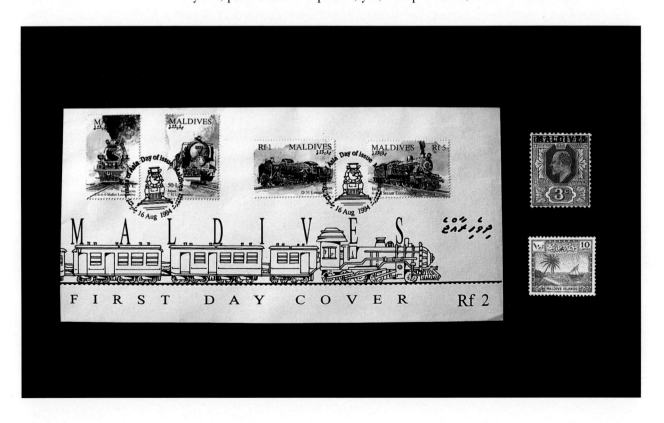

Fishy Business

How about hanging the jaws of a shark on the wall at home? It's an odd idea but shark jaws are a popular gift item available in souvenir shops or on the sidewalk outside Male's vegetable market. The rows of vicious looking teeth would certainly make a conversation piece, giving you a chance to talk about your Maldives holiday.

The take-home taste of the Maldives is available in the can of local tuna fish, in the dried fish chips and in the tuna paste, *rihaakuru*, sold in a plastic sachet.

Other edibles that are different souvenirs are the popular breadfruit chips, slithers of local breadfruit seasoned and fried. An almond-like nut called *kanamadhu* is a tasty snack. Or why not a whole coconut? All of these can be bought in the vegetable market in Male' or hygienically packed at the confectionery supermarket in the duty-free shopping mall at the airport.

Where local people shop is a good source of souvenirs. Small household implements make unusual gifts, especially since they are useful as well as decorative. A granite stone spice crusher complete with stone rolling pin may be too heavy to take home, but a small coconut scraper, coconut shell spoon or wooden mortar and pestle might suit instead. There are an amazing amount of locally used implements made from some part of the coconut, like coir fibre string or an ashtray.

The shops around the vegetable market where islanders go for their daily needs could yield items more typical of the Maldives than a T-shirt. It is there you will find the local hubble-bubble pipe, called a *guduguda* in Dhivehi because of the sound it makes when it is smoked.

Tortoise shell ware used to be produced and sold locally but since January 1996 a rigorous ban has been in force on turtle products. It is part of the campaign to let the turtle live in peace in the waters of the Maldives. Coral, too, should be left where it is. If it is never bought from the souvenir shop shelves, its plunder from the seabed might cease. And shells? Many of them are imported. You could always take home some money: the cowrie shells that used to be currency are sold in special boxes.

Today's money, the local bank notes, are very collectible. Each has an interesting local scene on one side and on the reverse the bow view of a lantern-rigged boat, called an *odi* in full sail. These boats were used to transport passengers and cargo up to the 1960s. Hold the note up to the light to see the state emblem depicted as the watermark.

The various values of telephone cards sold by Dhiraagu, the telephone company, have island views which make them sought after by card collectors. At least they don't take up much luggage space.

It is fun to hunt local souvenirs by yourself. There is no pressure to buy when you wander into a shop by yourself, and you may chance on something you have never seen before.

The State Trading Organisation (STO) shopping plaza in Orchid Magu has a supermarket where useful items like a rice spoon or a sarong can be bought. They are not made in the Maldives, but they are typical of the Maldivian way of life. However bizarre, if it reminds you of the Maldives, it is surely worth it.

Wish You Were Here: A Postcard Home

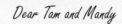

THE GUEST KNOWS BEST

The best person to write about a holiday in the Maldives is someone who is actually on holiday there. These extracts are from genuine postcards written by guests in island resorts.

Dear Tam and Mandy

As we sit here sipping a glass of champagne, watching the sun go down, I thought I would write a quick card from our hideaway island. It is truly glorious, the sun is hot, the sea is turquoise blue and we are having a very relaxing time. Bore you with photographs (hundreds of them!) on our return.

Lots of love, Sebastian & Tricia

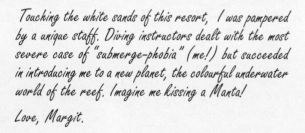

Touching the white sands of this resort, I was pampered by a unique staff. Diving instructors dealt with the most severe case of "submerge-phobia" (me!) but succeeded in introducing me to a new planet, the colourful underwater world of the reef. Imagine me kissing a Manta!

Love, Margit.

Dear Mum & Dad

Staff genuinely friendly, have relaxed us and put us at ease. Diving with whale sharks! Won beers at the Crab Races. Dancing on the beach, guitars, fish, coconuts, star-filled skies: magic! Got away and relaxed in "Heaven On Earth".

Love, Bill & Pamela

It's very relaxing under the tall palm trees, listening to the ruffling of leaves and the sound of the sea breathing on to the soft white sandy beaches. Great diving, snorkelling and surfing! Very friendly and helpful staff, excellent food...

Our best regards and thanks to all your employees: gardeners to dhoni crew, waiters to office managers... We are very pleased about the service we were able to enjoy. But the most important part to us in our holidays is always the contact with the human being. The knowledge of other cultures and languages...We are looking forward to meeting your nice staff again in the future. It was great fun. Thank you.

Bert and Freda

Dear Barbara

You'll never believe how beautiful this small island is. We stay in a very tasteful furnished bungalow which is well integrated in the natural surrounding. We go for snorkelling or diving nearly every day and you would be really impressed by the nice and intact house reef which is very close to the beach. We'll spend the whole day tomorrow as castaways on a coral island, just us!

Greetings from Bianca.

Dear Maldives

I remember you with nostalgia. Only there I had the feeling I could live the past again, I could live the present with no limits, I could live the future as I dreamt it. Thank you for the magic atmosphere.

Angelo

Towards the Future

Due Tribute

Many factors have contributed to the success of tourism in the Maldives. Parallel to the development of the industry has been an uplifting of standards of living for Maldivians, as a result of full employment. While the respect for religious and cultural values remains strong, the visitor is an honoured guest. Yet, although the Maldives depends on tourism for most of its foreign exchange, Maldivians are not subservient to the foreigners who are the source of that exchange. A stranger is welcomed graciously and left alone to holiday in peace.

Sustainable Development

In May 1996, the government announced the endorsement of the Second Tourism Masterplan for the country and its agreement that those recommendations in the Plan that could be implemented immediately should be carried out without delay.

The proposal of the masterplan is to increase the tourist bed capacity by 10,000 beds in the next 10 years. Further, the cabinet decided that as well as the already proposed development of tourism in Vilingili in Addu Atoll, tourism should be introduced to other regions where it can be developed in an economically viable manner.

The cabinet also endorsed the proposal made in the masterplan to form a Tourist Board. This Board will function under the Ministry of Tourism, and will have

Invest in Tourism

The Maldivian way of life has provided a firm foundation of unity and stability. Over the past two decades, the traditional economic life of subsistence agriculture and fisheries has been transformed into a market-driven, skills-based economy. The GDP growth is fuelled mainly by the success and expansion of the tourist industry.

The background is healthy for investment potential. The Foreign Investment Services Bureau of the Ministry of Trade, Industries and Labour is encouraging investors to consider the Maldives for real estate development, time-sharing homes, residential island development and in maritime industries like boat building and fisheries, as well as financial services, commercial infrastructural projects, mineral exploration, bunkering and commercial agriculture. The Ministry of Tourism is keen to work with investors in the expansion of tourism and support facilities.

Together with the natural advantages of the Maldives come fiscal benefits: 100% foreign investment, joint ventures, no taxes on personal income or corporate profits, no capital gains tax, no VAT; exemption of duty on imports, no exchange control and full repatriation of profits. Add the potential for high economic growth, political stability and a highly literate and keen workforce, with good labour relations and absence of strikes, and freedom to manage investments using foreign managerial, technical and manual employees, and you have the perfect country for profitable investment.

membership drawn from the private sector of the tourism industry, in addition to representatives from the government.

Commenting on the Masterplan in 1996, the Minister of Tourism, Ibrahim Hussain Zaki said: "We prefer to make 3,000 more beds available first, then we will review the situation over a couple of years. Ours is a cautious approach, but we are aware of the supply and demand of the situation."

Tourism is to be introduced into other atolls where transport and communication facilities make it feasible. Together with the improvement of the airport on the island of Gan in Addu Atoll, and the introduction of flights from overseas, via Male', this was seen as a way to sustain the benefits of tourism in parts of the Maldives where development is most needed. It would also take the pressure off Male' as the rather overwhelmed fulcrum of the existing industry.

Credit List

Many developments have taken place during the period of tourism. Health and social education has led to betterment of the standard of living, longer life span (child mortality has dropped dramatically) and responsible citizenship. Career training through further education, job options and career prospects have all improved.

Communications have kept pace with, and helped, the swift transition in 25 years from a somnolent past to a country energetically preparing for the 21st century. Television came to the Maldives in 1978 with the opening of Television Maldives (TVM). Maldivians have become part of the world community and aware of the advantages of life in the Maldives.

Access to good education is available nationwide and enthusiastically embraced. Combined with an English medium system is a system concentrating on the realities and culture of society to equip pupils for the modern world.

Children would surely find life in the rest of the world a contrast to their own. In the Maldives there is peace and stability: crime is low, so is inflation and the number of road accidents. The Republic of Maldives is unique, not only because of its unspoiled human and natural resources, but also for the good management that makes the preservation of those resources possible.

There is a lot to celebrate about 25 years of tourism in the Maldives. With the help of those who know and love the islands, and of concerned people around the world, the Maldives celebration can be a lasting holiday affair.

FURTHER READING

Anderson, Dr Charles: *Living Reefs Of The Maldives*
Bell, H. C. P.: *Monographs on the History, Archaeology and Epiography of the Maldive Islands*
Ellis, Royston & Amarasinghe, Gemunu: *Guide To Maldives*
Farook, Mohamed: *The Fascinating Maldives*
Gayoom, Maumoon Abdul: *Maldives: A Global View*

Heyerdahl, Thor: *The Maldive Mystery*
Maloney, Clarence: *People Of The Maldive Islands*
Maniku, Hassan Ahmed: *Islands Of The Maldives*
Maniku, H. A. & Dissanayake, J. B.: *Say It In Maldivian*
Mohamed, Amin and others: *Journey Through Maldives*
Neville, Adrian: *Male'–The Capital*

Royston Ellis is a distinguished author and travel writer who specialises in writing about Indian Ocean destinations for British and Asian publications. He has visited the Maldives regularly since 1983 and spent several months touring the atolls and resorts in 1994 and l995 researching for the widely-acclaimed book, *Guide to Maldives*. He is the author of bestselling guide books on India, Mauritius and Sri Lanka as well as of several historical novels written under the pseudonym of Richard Tresillian. A Life Fellow of the Royal Commonwealth Society, he often lectures on cruise liners about the Maldives and Indian Ocean countries. He is a resident of Sri Lanka.

Photo by Kumara Dayawansa

Gemunu Amarasinghe took up photography while at school in his home country of Sri Lanka, joining the *Sunday Times* of Colombo in 1990. He began freelancing in 1991, specialising in travel and architectural photography. His work has appeared in the *Daily Telegraph*, *Sunday Times* and *House & Garden* of the UK, and in the inflight magazines of Emirates, Gulf Air and Air Lanka. His photographs of Zanzibar, Seychelles, Reunion and Kenya have been featured in major travel magazines and he has contributed photography to guide books on India, Sri Lanka and Mauritius. He is the photographer, and co-author with Royston Ellis, of *Guide to Maldives*.

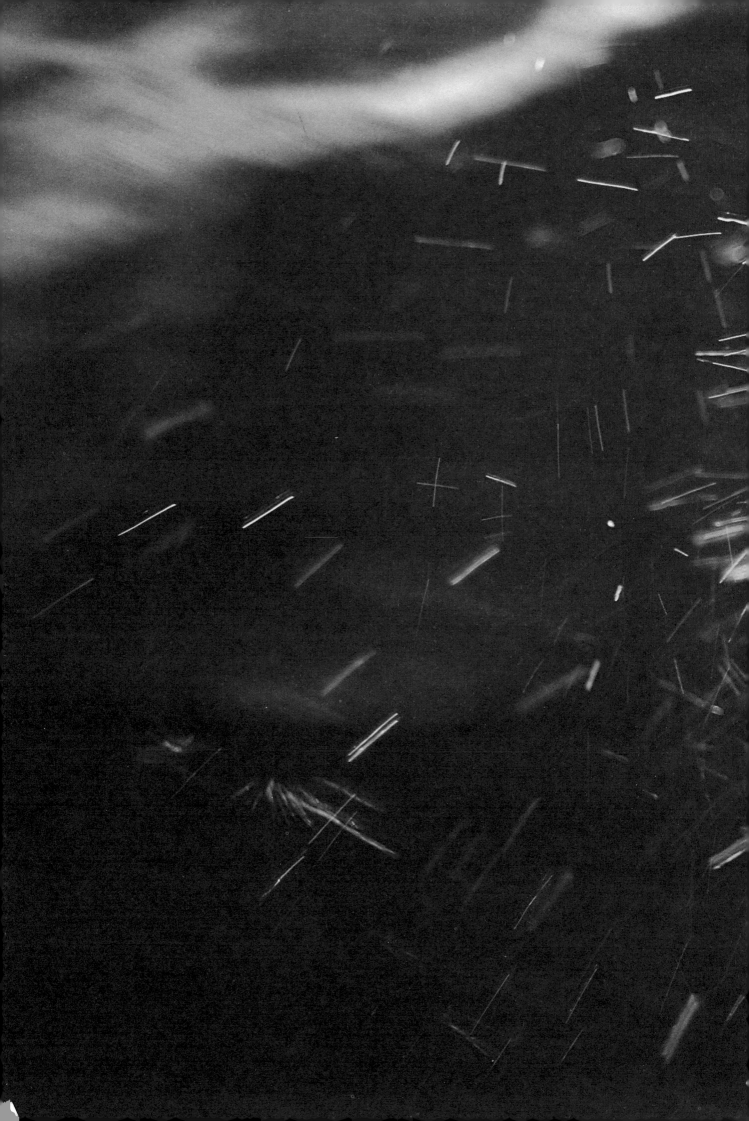